THE COLLECTOR'S GUIDE TO
PLAYING CARDS

MARK PICKVET

Schiffer Publishing Ltd®

4880 Lower Valley Road • Atglen, PA 19310

Dedication

To my mother and sister Juli, for relentlessly searching out rummage, yard, church, and garage sales for that odd deck of playing cards.

Other Schiffer Books by the Author:
The Encyclopedia of Glass. Volume 2. ISBN: 978-0-7643-3925-7. $29.99
Shot Glasses. ISBN: 978-0-7643-2079-8. $39.95

Other Schiffer Books on Related Subjects:
Gambling Collectibles: A Sure Winner. Leonard Schneir. ISBN: 978-0-8874-0541-9. $29.95

Copyright © 2013 by Mark Pickvet

Library of Congress Control Number: 2013954001

Cover design: Bruce Waters
Type set in Americana XBd BT/Arrus BT

ISBN: 978-0-7643-4482-4
Printed in China

Published by Schiffer Publishing, Ltd.
4880 Lower Valley Road
Atglen, PA 19310
Phone: (610) 593-1777; Fax: (610) 593-2002
E-mail: Info@schifferbooks.com

For our complete selection of fine books on this and related subjects, please visit our website at www.schifferbooks.com. You may also write for a free catalog.

This book may be purchased from the publisher. Please try your bookstore first.

We are always looking for people to write books on new and related subjects. If you have an idea for a book, please contact us at proposals@schifferbooks.com

Schiffer Publishing's titles are available at special discounts for bulk purchases for sales promotions or premiums. Special editions, including personalized covers, corporate imprints, and excerpts can be created in large quantities for special needs. For more information, contact the publisher.

Table of Contents

Bicycle Rider Backs

Acknowledgments

I wish to express my heartfelt gratitude to all of those people who had a hand in the development of this work. Collectors and dealers often allowed me to photograph or paw through their collections, if only to make a few notes. Fellow collectors and enthusiasts have sent me numerous photos (35mm and digital), scanned images, and even a few drawings/copies here and there. Family members have purchased cards for me in significant quantities, especially my mother, Lee Pickvet, and sister, Juli Pickvet. Aside from friends, family, fellow collectors, and dealers, there are always other people behind the scenes such as helpful and knowledgable editors, typesetters, photographers, printers, marketers, publishers, and computer experts in this day and age. I simply wish to thank you kindly and sincerely hope that I haven't forgotten anyone: Edward Becker, Jean Becker, John Berry, Douglas Congdon-Martin, Robert Darnold, Susan Darnold, Robert Davidson, Andrea Dubay, Edward Ferguson, Jill Ghattas, Anne Greene, Arthur Harshman, Ray Hartz, John Janssen, Andrea Kannon, Ward Lindsay, Mark Luca, David Madore, Rachel Moore, David Parlett, Fairy Pickvet, Kate Pickvet, Louis Pickvet Jr., Louis Pickvet III, Cathy Rex, Tim Rex, Lori Rivette, Erin Robinson, Ronald Robinson, Pete Schiffer, Peter Schiffer, Jill Smith, Kent Smith, Sandra Smith, Thomas Smith, William Smola, Jeffrey Snyder, Paul Traviglia, Beverly Viana, John Viana, Ann-Marie Warner, and Douglas Warner.

An Introduction to Collecting Playing Cards

The collecting of playing cards is another of those growing hobbies in the field of collectibles over the past couple of decades, especially with the advent of on-line auction services like eBay. The listings for cards alone at times exceeds 10,000, which puts it in line with such collectibles as Coca-Cola, dolls, bottles, shot glasses, and a variety of other highly popular but select antique/collectibles categories. You can find minimal listings in flea market companions and antique guides, which is one reason why I have tried to write a far more comprehensive guide. Playing cards have a rich and colorful history and one of the positive factors for collecting them is that they fit all budgets, from inexpensive modern styles to a few select antique examples that reach into the thousands. Typical new tourist and modern big-name advertising decks are priced low, as in the $2 to $6 range.

Playing cards are another one of those so-called "quantity" collectibles. Typical collectors start with a few, add a few more, a couple dozen turns into fifty, and sooner rather than later, one acquires their first 100! Once the word gets out, family and friends join in too. Playing cards can be found inexpensively at flea markets, garage and yard sales, and even antique stores. Another advantage is that their small size makes it possible to store many in a relatively small area; however, long-time collectors that I have run into typically only display a hundred or two of their best. A few have boxes and boxes of them stored away as one particular enthusiast I ran into has over 10,000! A word of caution on going overboard on quantity, many of the decks that hardcore collectors store away are those with localized advertising. Unless it has an impressive picture of a classic car or train or what have you, "Bob's Local Garage" or "Betty's Insurance Agency" or the local bank, real estate office, credit union, neighborhood store, auto repair garage or dealership, and so forth, are all virtually worthless. I once was the winning bidder on a lot of 40 decks of cards for $5 (it cost me about twice as much to have them shipped!), but there were only two decks I was really going for (one was a 1950s Hotpoint Kitchen Center deck and the other was a Coors Beer advertising deck). The rest, like many collectors, end up in a dusty box that is simply packed away.

One offshoot that seems to be more popular in England than in America is the collecting of single cards with a unique back design (mostly advertising). It's easier, if only for storage as they can be framed or placed in albums like sports cards and for variety's sake, to collect single cards rather than entire decks. Note that I have purposefully left out localized advertising decks in the price guide as I could have provided thousands of listings and perhaps put $0.10 down as a price. The same goes for the thousands of other somewhat generic designed card backs too (i.e. flowers, trees, animals, scenery, etc.). Also, I have focused on complete decks too though I do realize there is a little premium for certain single cards like jokers, aces (especially the ace of spades), and face cards. The ace of spades and jokers might sell for 10% of the deck, face cards and other aces a little less at about 7–8%, and the numbered cards mostly for their backs (5%). Even then, single cards are usually sold in lots for just a few dollars.

What I have tried to focus on is generally the most desirable area, and that is popular advertising at the national and even international level. Beware of reproductions out there too; like many popular collectibles, they have struck playing cards too! A few modern companies have produced reproductions of nineteenth century decks without indices and one-way face cards.

One way face cards, no indices.

They're fairly easy to spot since they often include a reprint or copy of the old tax stamps rather than the stamp itself; nevertheless, an occasional unscrupulous seller may try to pass them off as old (sometimes this is due to an honest or uninformed mistake). One thing to always be careful of is that if something looks too new, it just might be! Rarely is there a true antique deck of cards that hasn't been played with. Most, if not all, usually exhibit some telltale signs of age. Many of the "Spotter" decks for the armed forces have been reproduced as well. Beware of the word "Vintage" since it is mostly an undefined, or in the very least, a loosely defined term often passed off as old or antique when it could be just the opposite. Someone or some company that recently went out of business could now have "vintage products." "Vintage 1980" is really not that old!

"Antique" is another word that occasionally suffers some abuse. In the world of antiques and collectibles, a true "antique" is generally accepted as being something that is seventy-five years of age or older; nevertheless, there are always exceptions. Antique cars for instance are given the title at twenty-five years of age. Like "vintage," the word "antique" might mean or refer to something that isn't that old at all. For playing cards, seventy-five years is a good measure for antiques, but that doesn't stop misuse of the word.

Speaking of dating, there are quite a few factors involved. Prior to the 1870s, there were no jokers, no corner indices, and court or face cards were full-length body caricatures with legs and feet (not reversible or double-sided). Easy ones to date are those that have anniversary dates or were made for certain expositions like World's Fairs. Local advertising may have three, four, and five-digit telephone numbers prior to the widespread use of seven digits; likewise, before area codes and even zip codes were universally adopted. Knowledge of art, literature, culture, and politics of a particular era can, at times, be traced on playing cards (i.e. Civil War generals, presidents, military spotting cards, World War caricatures, patriotic messages, advertising slogans, pin-up art, clothing & hair styles, coal companies as opposed to oil companies, etc.). Early cards used wrappers instead of boxes; thus, many early decks lack a box or container. These wrappers were quite fragile and usually did not survive. Cards in slip cases were generally made from the very early 1900s up into the World War II era of the early 1940s. Early paper stock in card-making was somewhat coarse and not polished. Plastic coated cards do not appear in abundance until after this time. Those found in museums were even made of bone and leather but these do not often find their way into the

Reproduction Spotters.

GRAPHIC TRAINING AID   **44-2-10**
Cards 1-53

AIRCRAFT RECOGNITION PLAYING CARDS

DISTRIBUTION: To be distributed to
U.S. Army Training Aids Centers.

HEADQUARTERS, DEPARTMENT OF THE ARMY
Revision of GTA 44-2-6, October 1979

U.S. Army Issue Spotters.

collector market. Linen too was used as a supplement in the manufacture of card-based paper from about 1910 to 1940 (you can see the strands if you examine the cards closely). A handful used linen after 1940; however, the expense was quite prohibitive and all eventually discontinued its usage within a few short years.

Then, of course, up until 1965, as represented by a revenue stamp, cards were given a so-called "sin" tax like alcohol and tobacco. Religious institutions frowned upon them from their very beginning since they often involved gambling or mysticism (fortune-telling tarot cards). In the United States, the first such tax was applied on cards to help fund the Civil War in 1862. U.S. Post Office and Scott Stamp Catalog numbers include R2, R11, R12, R17, R21, R28, and Proprietary stamps RU1–RU16.

From 1862 to 1871, George Washington 1c, 2c, 3c, 4c, or 5c stamps were applied with "U.S. Inter. Rev." on top and "Playing Cards" at the bottom. From 1871 to 1883, a George Washington portrait in black with a blue border was pictured on the stamp with no special mention of playing cards. From 1883 to 1894, there was no tax. A new stamp act was enacted in August of 1894 and cards, until 1918, were just given a regular 2 cent common stamp. From 1918 to 1922, long vertical blue stamps with "Class A' in the center were applied to playing cards. From 1922 to 1924, the size was shortened to a smaller rectangular blue "Class A" stamp. From 1924 to 1929, the small rectangular blue stamp was changed to read "10 Cents" in the center. From 1929 to 1940, the stamp was lengthened again to a longer horizontal blue with "10 Cents" in the center. In 1940, it was briefly changed to a small rectangular blue "1 Pack" stamp and then again to a longer horizontal blue "1 Pack" stamp. The longer and most common version found lasted until the tax was repealed for good in 1965. Note, however, that many companies continued to make their own stamps, which still acted as a seal for the deck. One item to be wary of is the placement of newer cards in an older package—a stamp alone is not always the sole indicator of age! Older decks from the late nineteenth and early twentieth centuries were placed in slip covers and often they were used by regular folks to house newer and even older cards that did not have boxes or wrappers. Also note that the tax stamp did not have to be affixed until the actual deck was distributed, meaning that the deck could be older than the stamp.

For most early American decks, the ace of spades is the most important card when it comes to identification and even dating. Not only did it serve as the top or even double as a cover for the deck, it usually contains the manufacturer's name, the place of manufacture, and codes that at times can aid in dating. The United States Playing Card Company began using a coding system in 1904 at the bottom of the ace of spades utilizing a letter followed by four digits such as A4961 or Z7490. They recycled the letters too, roughly every twenty years, so other means are necessary for definitive identification (still, with a twenty-year gap, it isn't that difficult, especially if the revenue stamps are still present). 1904 (G), 1905 (H), 1906 (J), 1907 (K), 1908 (L), 1909 (M), 1910 (N), 1911 (P), 1912 (R), 1913(S), 1914 (T), 1915 (U), 1916 (W), 1917 (X), 1918 (Y), 1919 (Z), 1920 (A), 1921 (B), 1922(C), 1923 (E), 1924 (F), 1925 (G), 1926 (H), 1927 (J), 1928 (K), 1929 (L), 1930 (M), 1931 (P), 1932 (R), 1933 (S), 1934 (T), 1935 (U), 1936 (W), 1937 (X), 1938 (Y), 1939 (Z), 1940 (A), 1941 (C), 1942 ((D), 1943 (E), 1944 (F), 1945 (G), 1946 (H), 1947 (J), 1948 (K), 1949 (L), 1950 (M), 1951 (P), 1952 (R), 1953 (S), 1954 (T), 1955 (U), 1956 (W), 1957 (X), 1958 (Y), 1959 (Z), 1960 (A), 1961 (C), 1962 (D), 1963 (E), 1964 (F), 1965 (G), 1966 (H), 1967 (J), 1968 (K), 1969 (L), 1970 (M), 1971 (P), 1972 (R), 1973 (S), 1974 (T), 1975 (U), 1976 (B), 1977 (X), 1978 (Y), 1979 (Z), 1980 (A), 1981 (C), 1982 (D), 1983 (E), 1984 (F), 1985 (G), 1986 (H), 1987 (J), 1988 (K), 1989 (L), 1990 (M), 1991 (P), 1992 (R), 1993 (S), 1994 (T), 1995 (U), 1996 (W), 1997 (X), 1998 (Y), 1999 (Z), 2000 (A), and on and on.

Various card stamps.

During the late nineteenth century in America, cycling took the company by storm. Not motorcycles just yet, but leg-powered unicycles, bicycles, and tricycles. Russell & Morgan, the forerunners of the United States Playing Card Company, decided to produce a line of playing cards; however, they lacked a name for their product. They appealed to their employees, and a printer by the name of Gus Berens, came up with "Bicycle." The name was accepted and the famous Rider Back made its debut in 1887. Since then, it has featured dozens of different designs, but has never gone out of production. The traditional red or blue back exhibiting Cupid astride a two-wheeler is considered to be "The World's Favorite Playing Card," at least according to the U.S. Playing Card Company!

Another fascinating aspect about collecting playing cards is that the newer decks from about the 1970s on have much better art, photography, lithographs, pictures, graphics (now digitally mastered & enhanced), and in short, beauty, than older decks. One can easily compare the tourist decks of the 1950s and 1960s to modern designs to view significant differences—the prices are about the same for each too! As will be noted in the history section, trains or railroad-related cards always garner a lot of attention on auction sites; expect to pay more for these cards, since the demand is higher. Conversely, there are a lot of good buys to be had in advertising at present. Beer, liquor, cigarettes, air and cruise liners, cartoons, movies, soft drinks, motorcycles, and so forth can be had for as little as a couple of dollars. In this case, watch for postage/shipping rates; rarely should it cost more than that same couple of dollars to have a single deck of cards shipped within one country like the United States. Those that charge exorbitant rates like $5.95 or $6.95 are best avoided unless you really want that pack and it's the only one of its kind listed! Priority (two–three day delivery by the U.S. Postal Service) mail rates as of this printing are $5.15 for a pound, which equates to at least a good four decks of cards.

Conversely, if you are a seller, the best way to rid yourself of local advertising decks or non-advertising decks with generic designs, is to package them together in a bundle! If you have something in there that someone wants, then you'll get those bids. With thousands upon thousands of listings on eBay alone on any given day, many go unsold. Casino decks are a case in point. Every hour or two of use, casinos generally replace their cards. In the gambling mecca of Las Vegas, hundreds if not thousands of used decks each and every day are packed up—some casinos still punch holes in them—and then sold in gift stores, to flea market dealers, and are even auctioned off (occasionally you will find lots of hundreds listed on eBay). Some are given away as promotional items too. You can usually find used casino cards for $1 per deck and most are quality Bee or Paulson brands.

In conclusion, I believe that card-collecting is a growing hobby and that there are many great buys out there in advertising, many of which are likely to increase in value as the years go by. Thousands and thousands of card decks spring up on auctions every day, so, if you have a unique deck or recent discovery to share, drop me an email at Mpickvet@aol.com

A Brief History of Playing Cards

"Who cares for you?" said Alice, "You're nothing but a pack of cards!"
Lewis Carroll, *Alice's Adventures in Wonderland*

The predecessors of playing cards can be found in the realms of ancient gambling games. There is much historical evidence that games played with counters or pieces on a board were preceded by games in which the movement is completed by throwing dice or dice-like objects. Tossing sticks, bones, pieces of wood, nutshells, carved bone or ivory, or irregularly shaped multi-sided stones was apparent long before board games and counters. This was going on as far back as 3,000 B.C., especially in the ancient Orient and Africa, at least as far as the archaeological record is concerned. In many early games, such as the Egyptian Tab, the Korean Nyout, the East Indian Pachisi (Parcheesi), and Backgammon, the throwing of dice controlled the moves of the playing pieces upon some type of marked surface. As more of the element of chance was eliminated, games evolved into more highly defined measures of precise skill in such games as the Japanese Go, East Indian Chess, Chinese Wei-Kei, and English Draughts or Checkers. Of course, simple games like Nim or Tic-Tac-Toe still required the placement of pieces in an organized, controlled, and thoughtful fashion; nevertheless, they gradually evolved into the more highly complex games. As in games like chess, the pieces became more varied with higher and lower powers as they included royalty like cards.

Many games like chess and backgammon are thought to have their roots in the Near East, such as India. For chess, it is most likely true, but not backgammon. The legends of India tell of a gentleman of high order named Qaflan who supposedly created backgammon. Others credit the first Sassanian king named Ardshir, the ruler of Persia in the third century as the inventor of the game. Backgammon or similar type games date at least back to the first Greek and Roman civilizations. Plato refers to a game where dice are thrown and men placed appropriately after due consideration. The Romans named their version "*ludus duodecim scriptorium*" which translates to "the twelve-lined game." The games were very close to modern backgammon with a few modifications.

Though unproven without some room for doubt and/or speculation, the various numbers in the game are thought to represent time and movements of the earth and sun. The twenty-four points on a board might correspond to twenty-four hours in a day; the twelve points in each half represent the twelve months of the year; the thirty playing pieces refer to the average days in a month; and day and night are represented by the corresponding light and dark playing pieces. Even the opposite sides of a die should add up to seven, which are naturally the number of days in a week. Much is speculative; nevertheless, early humans were much closer to the forces of nature than we are today. The choosing of four suits for cards includes many of the same natural observations—the four seasons (spring, summer, winter, fall), the four primary directions (north, east, west, south), the four elements (earth, air, wind, and fire), and so on. Also note that there are fifty-two weeks in a year, coincidence?

Early backgammon and chess pieces were often found in red and black, two of the earliest, most recognized colors by humanity (i.e., black for night, hair, cave paintings from linseed oil, etc., and red for blood, mostly from the hunting and killing of animals). Red and black have always been a staple of both checkers and cards into modern times. Speaking of chess, it is by far one of the most intellectually advanced games ever invented. Rivals such as checkers involves strictly tactics, and Go is all strategy. Chess intertwines both strategy and tactics to different degrees, depending on each individual game. There is still controversy concerning the origin of chess, but most agree that it had its beginnings in India around the late sixth or very early seventh century. The original version "*Chaturanga*," which is the Sanskrit word for "four limbs" or "four-membered," contained the four basic components of the Indian Army (note the reference to "4" again). These included elephants, horses, chariots, and foot soldiers. The original moves were actually governed by dice and was played by four players in two partnerships (note again the similarity to playing cards) around an 8" x 8" square board.

From India, the game moved to Persia and was known in that region as *"Chatranj."* Persia was constantly invaded by the Moors or Arabs, which aided the game as it spread throughout the Arabic world. The Moors often served unwittingly as a cultural exchange between East and West, and the same holds true for the spread of playing cards. The rules for such games as well as the pieces like in chess, began their process of gradual change and alterations with their introduction to each new culture. In chess, only the Raja (king) and Counselor (queen) did not take part in the actual hand-to-hand combat until the ninth century. The king was naturally the supreme head of the army, while the counselor's or chief minister's primary task was to lead the troops on the board. Cards began with these same type of rankings, from the top dogs (the kings), to those who served them.

From the Arabian world, chess spread further into the north. In the early eleventh century, the Moors brought the game to the southern part of Spain on one of their raids. By the late eleventh century, the Vikings and French were carving their own unique chess sets. In the twelfth century, chess was brought to England by returning crusaders as well as from the mobile Vikings. The actions set into motion for chess were very similar to that for playing cards. As with many games, there is always speculation and debate as to who or what country was the actual place of origin. China and the Korean Peninsula make the argument that long, thin, narrow carved bamboo sticks, some with the images of warriors (the higher order or more powerful caricatures) first appeared in the Orient in the late tenth century. The card-like sticks were designed to teach military strategy to young nobles. Instead of single warfare between opposing red and black armies (i.e., chess and backgammon), cards have two differing red armies and two differing black armies for more intricate and complicated movements. Other than the colors and the number four, there is little relationship to Oriental stick-like cards and a modern deck of cards; yet, there seem to be some basic ideas here that spread back to the West, at least as far as Egypt.

Paper was invented in China and so-called "money cards" with suits of coins or coin-like dominoes were shuffled and played with. The cards may have been actual paper money and did contain four distinct suits: coins, strings of coins (why the Chinese once punched holes or minted coins with a center hole—to carry many on a string), myriads of strings, and tens of myriads. They were represented with ideograms, with numerals 2–9 in the first three suits, and in numerals 1–9 in the tens of myriads. Naturally, they were used for gambling, given the coin or money reference. Later, with the invention of Mahjong, these same coin-style markers or stylized dots, along with bamboo shoots, are pictured prominently on tiles. The Chinese *"p'ai"* is used to describe both paper cards and gaming tiles. Aside from Mahjong, these items are considered to be more related to dominoes than playing cards.

India has also made a claim that the invention of *"Ganjifeh"* or *"Ganjifa,"* colorful hand-painted round playing cards, were the predecessors of rectangular European cards. Ganjifa cards have intricate designs of Indian gods like Vishnu, but usually consist of eight to twelve suits, each sporting two dignitaries and ten numerals. Records of Ganjifeh have not been found before the sixteenth century, so it is accepted about everywhere outside of India, that western-style cards influenced them rather than the other way around.

At present, the most accepted origin of a fifty-two pack of playing cards divided into four distinct suits comes from a historian by the name of L.A. Mayer. Mayer discovered a pack of playing cards in the Topkapi Sarayi Museum in Istanbul in 1939. The discovery was mostly ignored until Mayer's work was republished posthumously in 1971 with pictures of most of the cards. A similar fragment of a card that matched these cards outlined by Mayer originated to the very late twelfth or early thirteenth centuries. These cards are known as "The Mamalukes of Egypt" and contain swords, polo sticks, cups, and coins as the four suits. Each suit contains cards with the numerals one through ten along with court cards labeled as *"Malik"* (king), *"Na'ib Malik"* (viceroy or deputy king), and *"Thani Na'ib"* (second or under deputy). Note that the court cards contained abstract designs with names only, not the profiles of people. The Arabic *"Na'ib"* for deputy is the origin of the Italian *"Naibbe"* and the Spanish *"Naipes,"* which quickly became "The Game of Deputies" or simply "Cards." The latin word *"charta"* refers to a sheet of paper that was soon written in various European languages as *cart, carta, carte, karte, karta, kartya,* and so forth. Any practical printing of cards required the widespread economical production of paper, which did not occur in regularity in the Western world until the thirteenth century. The first decks were hand-painted works of art, somewhat larger than modern playing cards.

As far as Europe goes, both Spain and Italy to this day lay claim to being the European originator of modern playing cards. Cards are first clearly mentioned in Spain in 1371 and in Italy within a year or two of that date. Since Venice was the most popular European trading port at the time, at least as trade moved from East to West and vice versa, cards likely passed through there first. Note that since polo was unknown by Europe in the fourteenth century, the Italians changed the polo sticks in their suits to batons. Not to be outdone, the Spanish used cudgels, which eventually became clubs. In 1377, cards are mentioned in detail by John of Rheinfelden, a monk of Switzerland in his famous quote: "Thus it is that a certain game, called the game of cards, has reached us in the present year, namely AD 1377." Within a few short years afterward, they had spread throughout the major cities of Europe. John of Rheinfelden is also credited with this passage on cards that comes from a manuscript copy made in 1429:

In the game called cards, the cards are painted in different designs and are played with in various ways. In the commonest manner—the one in which they first reached us—four cards depicts four kings, each of whom is seated upon a royal throne. Each of them holds a certain sign in his hand, some of these signs being considered good but others signifying evil. Under these kings comes two marshals, of whom the first holds the sign upwards, as the king does, but the other holds the sign downwards in his hand. After this are ten other cards, of the same overall size and shape. The king's sign appears once on the first of these, twice on the second, and so on with the others up to and including the tenth. Thus the king is the thirteenth card, and there are fifty-two cards altogether.

Note that John does not provide us with the suit signs used; however, it does give us reference to the original meaning of "Over" and "Under" in regard to the ranking of the respective male figures who serve the king. Also note that there is no mention of jokers just yet either. About the time of John's copied work (early fifteenth century), France, Germany, and Switzerland quickly became the leaders in card production in later Medieval Europe. In terms of design, the manufacturers made up their own rules as the selection of suits and face cards or courts as they were originally known. Original packs were created with individually stenciled cards, woodblock, and metal engraving while the suits were chosen from just about anything, mostly from nature and everyday life: animals, acorns, banners, batons, bears, bells, candles, cannons, clovers, coins, columbine, crowns, cupids, cups, deer, ducks, eagles, falcons, flowers, goats, hares, harps, helmets, herons, horses, keys, leaves, lilies, millstones, nuts, parrots, paving stones, pence or pennies, pinks, pikes, purses, rabbits, rings, roses, sheep, shields, shovels, stags, swords, thimbles, and so on.

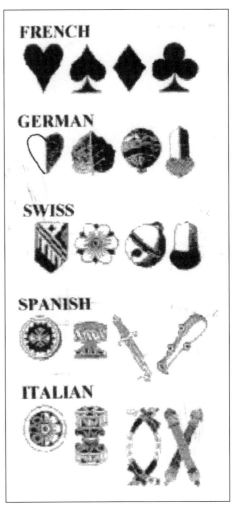

Various European suits. *Courtesy of the International Playing Card Society.*

The first card makers and painters combined their skills for painting and wood engraving to adorn them, especially in the towns of Ulm, Nuremburg, and Augsburg in the first half of the fifteenth century. Many early woodcuts were colored more efficiently with stencils, especially where quantity production was desired. The early court cards varied about as much as the suit choices too. The higher ranked (over) and lower ranked (under) marshals were mostly knights or chevaliers (over), and knaves or servants (under), who served the higher ranking king; however, the knaves ("*valet*" in French) were at times replaced with maidens. Queens made their appearance too in the mid-fifteenth century and in some German decks (from the 1440s), queens headed up their own suits, usually in two of the four suits, in place of kings. A few fifty-six-card packs were born as well in the fifteenth century complete with the king, queen, knight, and a valet. Obviously they didn't last long. Standardization was already in the works by the later fifteenth century.

Around 1480, French makers introduced the simple yet abstract shapes of spades, hearts, clubs, and diamonds. There is one legend that the four basic suits were derived from the four basic estates of the feudal or medieval system—military, peasantry, clergy, and bourgeoisie. Practically speaking, the designs could be brush-stroked simply and economically with a single stencil. The shapes could be made roughly the same size too. Spades were modeled after a simple all wooden shovel that was spade-tipped with iron for digging. Clubs were borrowed mostly from the Spanish, which is derived from an ordinary three-leaf clover or *trefle* (the trefoil leaf). The stylized heart symbol was borrowed from the German "*roth*" suit, which simply means red. The four-sided diamond shape is thought to have originated from a common similarly shaped paving stone. The designs have been traced to Rouen, a prolific manufacturing center in France, beginning in the very late fifteenth and early sixteenth centuries.

The French are also credited with ranking the court cards as king, queen, and valet, which is far more easily distinguished from a king and two underlings; hence, the elimination of the over and under ranking officers. Another legend is that France,

especially Paris, the hub of French culture, is a place of romance, and the addition of a queen, second to her king, promotes a more harmonious family grouping. It is these French-based suits and court cards that eventually found their way to England and America, but not to the rest of Europe. Frenchman Pierre Marechal, in 1565, is generally credited with producing the basic French designs of the court cards that were copied and altered somewhat by later English and American makers.

Not everyone followed the French. Then and now, German/Austrian decks sport hearts, acorns, leaves, and bells (round hawkbells). In Switzerland, it is shields, roses, bells, and acorns. In Spain and parts of Italy (Adriatic region), coins, cups, swords, and batons are used. Note that many of these other European style decks do not have queens (for instance, the German "*Ober*" and "*Unter*" rank under the king respectively); as you can see, these nations all contain their own cultural courts, separate and distinct from those invented by the French. Listed here are the more modern American/English court conversions as compared to the popular French designs representing the models or more simply the people on the playing cards:

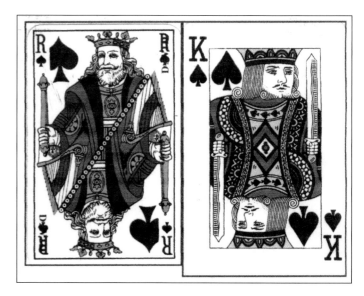

The King of Spades is the biblical King David, the slayer of Goliath. On the French card, he holds a scepter in one hand and a harp below it, and faces slightly to the left. On our modern card, he holds a sword and faces to the right.

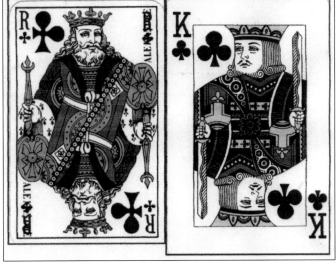

The King of Hearts is usually attributed to Charlemagne (Charles the Great) or could also be the French King Charles VII. He holds a sword and faces to the right. On our modern card, he holds a sword above his head (nicknamed "The Suicide King" for this gesture) while his other hand is also visible. He faces forward to the left; however, there is one distinction that he lacks that the other kings do not, and that is a moustache.

The King of Clubs is "Alexandre" in French for Alexander the Great. On the French card, he holds a scepter with shield, and faces mostly forward if slightly right. On our modern card, he holds a sword along with an imperial orb. His face also faces forward and a little to the left.

The King of Diamonds is modeled after Julius Caesar. On the French card, he really has no distinguishing attributes (i.e., no weapons, no visible hands, or symbols) and faces right. On our modern card, he is "The Man with the Ax," has a hand sticking out, and faces fully to the left.

The Queen of Spades is "Pallas" on the French deck for the Greek goddess Athena (also known as Minerva). She holds a tulip-like flower and faces directly left. On our modern card, she is the only queen with a scepter and faces forward and slightly to the right.

The Queen of Hearts is Judith of the "Book of Judith," an Apocryphal Book of the Bible. She holds a rose-like flower on the French deck and faces forward, slightly left. She faces in a similar fashion on the modern card while holding a stylized royal flower.

The Queen of Clubs is called "Argine" on the French card, an anagram of "Regina" meaning queen. She could also be based on or related to Hera's (Greek goddess) statue at Argos. Also on the French card, she is the only queen that does not hold a flower and faces a little to the right. On our modern card, she holds a stylized flower similar to the other queens and faces slightly to the left.

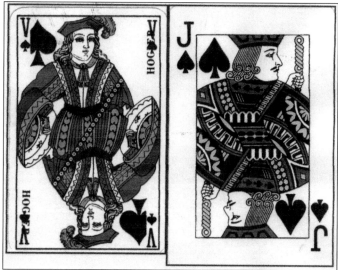

The Queen of Diamonds is based on Rachel, another biblical character; however, there is another legend that it is a corruption of the Celtic Ragnel (related to Lancelot). Rachel is also a pseudonym for mistress. On the French deck, she holds a poppy-like flower and faces a little to the right. On the modern card, she faces mostly left and holds a stylized flower.

The Jack of Spades is called "Hogier" on the French deck after Ogier the Dane from the "Song of Roland" (one of Charlemagne's cousins and paladins). On the French card, he sports a feather in his hat and faces slightly to the right. On the English deck he is one of the two "One-Eyed" Jacks along with the Jack of Hearts. Since he faces completely to the right, only one of his eyes is visible. He also holds a spiraling scepter and sports a moustache on the modern card.

The Jack of Hearts is called *"La Hire"* and refers to a famous French warrior, Etienne de Vignolles, a companion of Joan of Arc. He faces forward on the French deck a little to the right with face slightly pointed downward. On our modern card, he is the second of the "One-Eyed Jacks" and faces completely left with only one eye visible. He also has an ax behind his head and a moustache.

The Jack of Diamonds is "Hector" on the French deck but it is only sometimes attributed to the famous Hector of Troy (the Trojan hero immortalized by Homer). There is another Hector who was supposedly a companion brother of Lancelot. He faces completely right on the French card with only one eye visible. On our modern card, both eyes are visible as he faces slightly to the left. He also holds the longest visible sword of all face cards on the modern deck.

The Jack of Clubs is named after the Arthurian hero, Sir Lancelot. He sports a shield on the French deck and faces forward, if slightly to the left. Another legend indicates that the Jack of Clubs was modeled after Judas Maccabeus who led the Jewish rebellion against the Syrians; however, Lancelot is the more accepted. On the modern card, he holds what could be a staff or an arrow, but clearly not a sword. There is also a feather sticking from his hat and he faces forward, somewhat to the right.

The Medieval Era was one in which the various religious orders fought and soon split into many different factions. At the time, they did have a greater hold or say in politics as the threat of excommunication held some weight. The Reformation prior to the Renaissance era was Europe's foremost Western movement in the fifteenth and sixteenth centuries. Cards were at times unfairly associated with improper and illegal gambling and witchcraft (Tarot cards invented in the fifteenth century were improperly associated with Gypsies, who were not even in Europe at the time of their invention). The occult was not a good thing to be associated with, especially during such reigns of terror as the Spanish Inquisition. Certainly cards could be used for gambling and for fortune-telling; yet, they could also be no different from a pleasant form of entertainment like other board and dice games. The clergy often dubbed cards as tools of the devil and fought to have them outlawed and burned, not to mention punishment for those who played with them. Most of recorded history informs us that many a deck of cards was burned by religious zealots well before witches were burned! It didn't help matters that the number thirteen, associated with the suits, was grounds for suspicion as well.

Another legend has it that Christopher Columbus, on his famous voyage of America in 1492, ran into some violent storms in the Atlantic as he approached the Caribbean. The weather was blamed on God, angry and punishing them for playing cards (the tools of the devil) on the voyage. To appease His anger, several crewmen tossed the cards overboard. Apparently a few washed upon shore; thus, becoming the first cards imported to America! By this time, cards had quickly passed from the artworks made specifically for the nobility to cheaper versions for commoners and peasants. Naturally, the kings, princes, landlords, and other nobility of the later Middle Ages agreed with the Church and felt that cards were turning the working classes away from hard work and into the dangerous area of idleness. Of course, this wasn't the case within their own class or station! Unwittingly, cards became part of a class struggle pitting commoners against their lords and bishops. Since Church and State often went hand-in-hand in medieval times, even this formidable front could not contain the popularity of cards once they hit the general masses.

In the early games, the kings were always the highest ranking card in a suit. Who could possibly challenge the likes of King David, Charlemagne, Caesar, and Alexander? Why the lonely one-card of course! As early as the late 1400s, there was some special significance placed on nominally lowest card, it was "The One". What could be higher than "The One?" Many legends came about, and some have their roots in religion. "The One" could be the Judeo-Christian God and nothing could possibly outrank the power of the omnipotent or one true God. Another story comes from the French Revolution of the later 1700s whereby the concept of "Ace-High" is nothing more than a symbol of the lower classes who rise up in power and overthrow their kings or royalty in general. The face or court cards had almost always represented royalty in one form or another. The word "ace" itself is derived from the Latin *as* indicating the smallest unit of coinage.

Not to be outdone by the French, the English jumped on the card bandwagon and produced a wide range of playing cards in the late seventeenth and early eighteenth centuries. Most were idiosyncratic in nature as design after design was applied at the whim of the painter, cutter, or printer. No particular or universal version really caught on anywhere until they somewhat copied and slightly altered the French standards. A 1628 ban on the importation of foreign cards by England left English block-cutters to their own devices to create cards, many were not pretty! In the nineteenth century, Germany and Austria were noted for producing some of the most beautifully designed art-like cards for use in card games in polite society. Some of these fanciful models can be found on modern cards made by the Austrian Platnik company. A few examples are pictured here:

Mid-eighteenth century French examples.

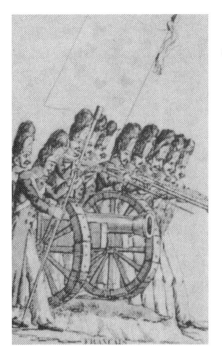

Game of French Flags, 1815.

Mid-nineteenth century Italian examples.

Swiss, nineteenth century.

Louis XV of France, ca. 1890.

English, nineteenth century.

French Transformation, late nineteenth century.

Speaking of England, the most famous name ever associated with cards came about in the eighteenth century. Edmond Hoyle, whose death is listed in 1769, was apparently born in the late 1600s or early 1700s as there is no official or surviving record of his birth. During his time, the card game of "Whisk" was arguably the most popular in England. Like a dance or piano instructor, Hoyle offered his services as a personal Whisk instructor or tutor to the upper classes; furthermore, he wrote a treatise on the game providing both rules and strategy. He sold copies of the manuscript for one guinea each, along with an additional guinea for personal tutoring. One guinea wasn't that expensive for the aristocrats;

nevertheless, the game was popular with the masses too and few could afford such a price. As a result, it was readily plagiarized as other unscrupulous dealers sold it for less. In an attempt to protect his interests, Hoyle had it officially copyrighted at Stationers' Hall in November of 1742, and it was published by Thomas Osborne in book form.

Up until this time, there had been various unpublished treatises, essays, guidelines, rules, and so forth on various card games throughout Europe, but none quite so popular as those by Hoyle. There were no significant books or compilations, however. Hoyle's first book went through five editions in its first year of publication alone and it was still widely pirated despite his, and the publisher's, efforts to combat it. In 1743, Hoyle became a celebrity as his tutoring services were in great demand for years and years to come. He continued writing and followed up the success of his first book with more on cards as well as other games too: Backgammon in 1743, Piquet and Chess in 1744, Quadrille in 1745, a compendium in 1750, Brag in 1751, and Chess exclusively in 1761. Ironically, most of Hoyle's works do not include rules, but simply strategies and tips for the beginner.

When Edmond Hoyle died in 1769, a huge variety of authors and publishers in England, as well as America, attached themselves to his namesake as rule book after rule book was printed. All include games that Hoyle had never played or even heard of, some were even invented after his death! "The Rules According to Hoyle" is still a popular quote today; nonetheless, there are at least a hundred versions with "Hoyle" in the title. One can easily find contradictions in the differing volumes. Since there are so many versions of certain games, it is best to agree upon them prior to starting a game of cards. Those who play in professional tournaments such as Bridge, Poker, Euchre, or what have you, use the rules officially sanctioned by the governing body or the sponsor itself as you likely aren't able to find anything to do with Hoyle! As a side note, about the only legitimate patent with the name Hoyle is the card brand produced currently by Hoyle Products, based in St. Paul, Minnesota—you can get them in both standard and pinochle versions.

Hoyle brand examples, Pinochle and Standard.

The later nineteenth century was also a time when many of the face or court cards were altered or replaced with figures from literary, historical, mythological, political, educational, and cultural figures, plus the first use of both contemporary and humorous figures as well. You might find Joan of Arc as a queen in a French deck, Shakespeare as a king in an English Deck, or perhaps Machiavelli as a jack in a German pack. Speaking of "pack" and "deck," the former is common in England (since the seventeenth century) today while the latter is most used in America. For some other languages, decks, packs, or cards are "*balicek*" in the Czech Republic, "*cartes*" in France, "*carts*" in Romania, "*csomag*" in Hungary, "*kaartspel*" in Dutch, "*kartenspiel*" in German, "*korona*" in Russia, "*mazzo*" in Italy, "*spil kort*" in Denmark, "*talia*" in Poland, and "*trapoula*" in Greece. The legendary transformation decks came out of this later nineteenth century era too. Those with such masterful and incredible drawings from card to card, appear to move or animate like a moving picture as the deck is flipped in a specific order. Each card is unique and drawn specifically to flow in an animated sequence. These are some of the most sought after and valuable decks around and can fetch prices in the thousands of dollars.

Due to religious admonitions, early American colonists, especially those of the Puritan variety, did not bring cards with them. Later colonists did, however, especially those from England in the early to mid-1700s. At that time, production was in full swing throughout Europe, including England. It was only a matter of time that they would spread overseas given the diverse nationalities that migrated to the New World. It wasn't until after the Revolutionary War that the American playing card industry got

established, mostly in the East Coast cities of Philadelphia, Boston, and New York. Beginning in the 1790s, there are records for Jazaniah Ford and Amos Whitney, who made cards in Massachusetts. Records for Philadelphia date to the same time period. New York printers followed in the very early 1800s. Up into the Civil War era, American decks contained full one-way face cards, no indices, and portraits basically like those of French and English makers. Few survive prior to the Civil War; however, good old Yankee ingenuity found its way into the card industry soon afterward. Listed here is a deck of cards prior to 1870 with one face cards and no indices:

EXPORTATION
I·HARDY·

Modern cards with corner indices.

One of the most simple and useful inventions on playing cards was the American invention of providing corner indexes or indices around the early 1870s. Some American manufacturers like Dougherty used miniature cards in the corners, which were called "Triplicates." A rival firm, the New York Consolidated Card Company, used numbers and called them "Squeezers," which won out as the industry standard. Since non-indexed cards often required both hands to hold them, the advantage of squeezers was and is that they may be scrunched or squeezed together in one hand. The innovation proved extremely popular and spread to Europe in a heartbeat.

One immediate consequence of adding indices was that the "J" for "Jack" became a permanent fixture in place of the "Kn" for Knave, the lowest ranking face or court card. "Kn" was confused with "K" for the King when the cards were squeezed together in a hand. Since the early 1600s, the Knave had often been nicknamed the Jack, mostly as a term borrowed from a card game called "All Fours." In All Fours, the Knave in trump was called the Jack. Since All Fours was considered a peasant or low-class game, the use of the word "Jack" was considered somewhat rude, vulgar, or beneath one's station. With the confusion between "Kn" and "K," Americans had no qualms about making the permanent change to Jack!

Corner indices had another advantage with the first tourist decks produced in the very late nineteenth and early twentieth centuries in America. Railroads and rail travel were the most common as most sported fifty-two different pictures of scenery or the trains themselves with nothing more than the corner indices to indicate what the card's rank and suit is. Other decks provided pictures of national parks like Yellowstone and it wasn't long afterward that a variety of wildlife (animals, birds, etc.), views, works of art, cartoons, other modes of transportation (cars, planes, boats, trains, etc.), pinups, beverages (beer, soda, and hard liquors), and naturally hot tourist spots like Las Vegas carried a similar format. If you fight for such older (early to mid-twentieth century for the most part) cards as the railway scenery on such auction sites as eBay, be prepared to go up against ferocious bidding for them! Most came in a leather carrying case once known as a hard slipcase too, with lettering. Even standard decks with railroads on them are hot sellers, certainly more so than airlines and cruise ships. Up into the early 1980s, airliners and cruise ships gave away decks of cards freely as part of their advertising promotions.

Another American invention in the 1870s is that of the joker. In one version of Euchre, it serves as the best bower over the other two. Since the game was sometimes referred to as "Juker," one story has it that the best bower card may have been called "The Juker," which eventually evolved into "Joker." Although the joker bears the image of a court jester, clown, jocular imp, or fool, with the fool being one of the images in Tarot cards, it is believed that there is little relationship between the two. Often, the jokers are different colors (usually red and black),

Jokers.

and one may be a bit more colorful and intricately detailed than the other (in a few odd games, the more elaborate one outranks the other). In most games where they are used, they hold the same power; however, in many games they're simply discarded and not used at all. Unlike face cards, the design of jokers varies widely as many manufacturers use them to carry their own specific trademarks. Note that a few early decks of the late nineteenth century were made with only one joker while other card decks from the late nineteenth and early twentieth centuries lack jokers even though they were produced with two. This happens for two reasons. One reason is that there used to be a good deal of joker collectors from this time period (less so today, but there are some still out there). Secondly, since most card games really do not require the use of a joker, many simply had no use for them and tossed them out! Their regular usage are only found in a few such select games such as poker, where jokers are sometimes used as wild cards, and canasta, where four are required in the standard double deck version. In canasta, the jokers, along with the deuces, also serve as wild cards; but note that the jokers are assigned a higher point total (usually fifty points as opposed to twenty for the twos).

The 1870s is often considered the last time that major and significant improvements were made to playing cards. Not only did Americans add corner indices and jokers, but about this same time period, the innovation of reversible face cards appeared too. Reversible court or face cards meant that players no longer had to turn upside down cards face up. With reversibles, it was impossible to be upside down! Before this invention, unscrupulous players could often get a hint of what the other players' hands contained by peaking at them as they reversed their cards! More reversals meant more face cards! Naturally, this new invention required the abandonment of the designs of the earlier full-length court cards. Yankee ingenuity did not stop there as further improvements in basic durability soon proved the superiority of American decks. By the later nineteenth century, American decks contained varnished surfaces for inhibiting wear, not to mention smoothness of shuffling, and rounded corners that avoided the problem of easily bent squared-off decks. Eventually, varnish gave way to plastic-coated finishes in the mid-twentieth century.

So, where does that leave us today? The primary or standard deck of cards that one purchases most anywhere in the world is fifty-four cards (though some European decks like the beautiful Piatnik cards provide three jokers for a total of fifty-five). Despite all of the novelty decks out there, when serious card players gather for gambling, tournaments, or simply for fun, it's the versions established centuries ago that we play with. The standard fifty-four-deck is sometimes called "Anglo-American Playing Cards," which includes thirteen ranks of four suits, spades, hearts, diamonds, and clubs. These are the universally accepted Unicode symbols for them from U+2660 to U+2667:

The Unicode standard defines 8 characters for card suits, from U+2660 to U+2667:

Unicode Standards.

on opposite corners only (rarely on all fours corners as the originals or some specific casino decks). Jumbo indices aid those with poor eyesight. A few other European differences include German decks that sport yellow or orange diamonds and green spades for further color differentiation. Naturally, many traditional Germans and Austrians still play with hearts, bells, leaves, and acorns in lieu of hearts, diamonds, spades, and clubs. Spain does have a special modern deck called *Brisca* with suits of *Bastos* (clubs), *Espadas* (swords), *Oros* (gold), and *Copa* (cups); it is used in Spain and a few other select countries with Spanish influence or Spanish-speaking populations (i.e., The Philippines, Puerto Rico, etc.).

One-eyed Jacks and The Man with the Ax.

As mentioned previously, there are some nicknames for certain cards. The Jack of Spades and the Jack of Hearts are the "One-eyed Jacks" since they are the only face cards, with the exception of the King of Diamonds, drawn in profile. They are at times called as wild cards in games like poker. The term "Acey, Deucy, One-eyed Jack" also includes aces and twos as wild cards too. "The Suicide King" is the King of Hearts since he appears with a broadsword behind or somewhat through his head. The King of Diamonds is "The Man with the Ax" and is sometimes called wild along with the "One-eyed Jacks." "Deuces" are of course twos while "Treys" are threes. Out of all the various nicknames, none may be more notorious than "The Death Card," the ace with the massive ornate spade, perfect for chopping heads!

Reversible face cards.

The courts or face cards are reversible Rouennais models along with two usually distinguishable jokers (if only in color). The individual cards number from one to ten depicted by as many pips or symbols. Note that modern playing cards carry index labels

Ace of Spades—the Death Card. Nineteenth century English deck.

Out of all the aces, the Ace of Spades stands out the most. Much of it is due to King James I of England. James passed a law requiring the insignia on the Ace of Spades specifically as proof of payment of a tax on the local manufacture of cards. It required the manufacturer's patented logo on this particular card along with the name of the printer. This was mandatory on all cards produced in the United Kingdom until it was repealed on August 4, 1960. Similarly in America, the revenue stamp was required until 1965. To this day, like jokers, many companies have their own unique patented Ace of Spades' design. Next to missing jokers, this is the card that one will most likely find missing in an incomplete deck! Note that Spades tend to be a higher ranking suit in such games as Bridge and Spades. Aside from jokers and the Ace of Spades, patents mostly exist for the card back design (i.e., USPCC's "Bicycle" or "Riderbacks" and Brown & Bigelow's "Shellback"). You'll find many in the pricing section. Pictured here on many uniquely patented Aces of Spades:

There are still fortune tellers out there today who use Tarot cards for soothsaying and making predictions. Even in our more enlightened times of the twenty-first century, there is still some influence exercised by various religious factions over cards. Take it from a long-time math instructor, there are people in the Western world who are not familiar with cards. The most prevalent reason is that their parents forbade them because they are still considered "the tools of the devil" by some. It seems that they will never shake off the onus of gambling and the negative aspects associated with it. In a math course, they are simply a prop used to study statistics and probable outcomes, mostly from the teachings of Pascal, who is well regarded as the Father of Probability Theory (seventeenth century). I personally taught a year at a private Catholic school once where cards were banned because of parental outcry. In the Muslim world, cards are also outlawed by many fundamentalist sects, as are many items in Western culture. Recall, however, that the Moors once served as a go-between from East to West. Many games may not have reached the West until much later without their influence.

On the flip side, cards are so ingrained in Western, and even Far Eastern, culture that they have become accepted standards for game playing for centuries, as we have seen. Playing cards are sometimes referred to as standard bridge or poker size (in Japan, it's a "Trump Deck"). Though they differ a little in width, you'll find most standard decks in the 3 ½" x 2 ½" range—see the price guide below for decks based on other dimensions. Today, an enviable amount of card variations have permeated about everything known in society, aside from those mentioned above, including popular movies, television, cartoons, books, magazines, news, computers, models, dolls, toys, action figures, tractors, presidents, generals, wars, comedians, authors, beverages, and on and on! One need only look at some of the pictures in this book to get an idea of the variety out there. Of course, in the greater name of advertising, there is no other single medium that has had so much effect on card back designs than those wishing to represent their products.

General Price Guide

What's it worth? There is likely no more frequently asked question than this when it comes to antiques and collectibles. Listed here is a guide to general prices by category. Please note that these are only estimates, as more exacting prices are listed under the following "Main Pricing Guide." As with all pricing guides, these values only serve as a general reference. They are not intended to set prices; rather they are determined from hundreds of listings from shows, auctions, dealers, mail-order catalogs, and collectors. Neither the author nor the publisher assumes responsibility for any losses that might possibly be incurred as a result of using this guide. The purpose of this book is to provide the most up-to-date and realistic prices for complete decks of playing cards.

There are many factors involved in pricing both antiques and collectibles, not the least of which are age, condition, demand, availability, and other relevant factors. Take special note that dealers only pay half the quoted prices listed in most pricing guides, and that is as long as they have an interest in the items, too. They pay even less for larger collections. The prices listed are what one would on average likely have to pay a dealer, antique store, or on the retail market for newer items.

MIB stands for "Mint in Box." This is a brand new deck that has never been opened. That means the seal is in place, the box is perfect, and it may still be wrapped in its original cellophane packaging if issued that way. If it was given a stamp, then the stamp has not been broken. Antique cards are simply not found in this condition, with rare exceptions.

NEW indicates that the seal may have been broken but the cards have not been played with. The cards should be in crisp, shiny, new condition without any bent corners, blemishes, stains, and so forth. Note that older cards on coarser paper or linen will not have a sheen (it is difficult to find these that have not been used in some way).

GOOD stands for a deck that has been played with. The cards will be worn some from play; however, they still should not be significantly creased, stained, or stuck together. Those that are damaged reduce the price significantly, though a little leeway is given for true antique decks (those seventy-five years of age or older) as long as they are completely intact (all fifty-two cards plus whatever

jokers were originally issued; forty-eight cards for Pinochle Decks). A missing or damaged box reduces the prices by about 10–15% as well. A missing card or two is devastating and usually halves the value or reduces it even more than 50% at times.

STYLE has some unique letter codes in it as follows:

DD represents a double deck set (prices are for both decks included together).

J is for a jumbo rectangular deck (larger dimensions than a single deck).

M is for a typical mini-deck (about 2 ¼" x 1 ½").

P is for forty-eight-card Pinochle Decks.

R is for a round or circular deck (usually 3" in diameter).

S is for a standard deck (usually 3 ½" or 3 5/8" x 2 ½").

T is for tiny decks (smaller dimensions than mini's).

TD represents a triple deck set (prices are for all three decks included together)

U is a deck with unusual dimensions.

As noted in the introduction, partial decks are worth far less. For single card collectors, the joker and ace of spades might get you as much as 10% of the value as the complete deck. Other aces and face cards 7–8%, and all other cards about 5%. Please note once again that these are only estimates and that single card collectors are usually looking for sharp colors in popular advertising (though there are a few that focus on animal-designed backs). Many one-of-a-kind items or oddities like those late nineteenth century transformation decks (the Holy Grail for card collectors!) are a bit harder to classify. Many depend on the elaborateness and uniqueness of the design or perhaps on the last time they were sold and/or auctioned off.

Nineteenth century French transformation—child swings and bicycles move as cards are flipped.

GENERAL PRICE GUIDE

CONDITION

DESCRIPTION	MIB	NEW	GOOD	STYLE
Airlines	$5.00	$4.00	$2.50	S
Beer	$8.00	$6.00	$4.00	S
Brands, Antique (75 years or older)			$50.00	S
Brands (I.e. Bicycle, Hoyle, Maverick, etc.), Modern	$1.50	$1.00	$0.75	S
Casinos	$2.00	$1.50	$1.00	S
Cigarettes	$6.00	$4.50	$3.00	S
Congress, Double Deck Sets in Marked Cases, 1950s–1970s	$8.00	$6.00	$4.00	DD
Cruise Ships, Big Ships	$6.00	$4.50	$3.00	S
Cruise Ships—Lettering/Logos	$4.00	$3.00	$2.00	S
Department Stores	$10.00	$7.50	$5.00	S
Fastfood Restaurants	$12.00	$9.00	$6.00	S
Generic Designs (I.e. flowers, animals, scenery, etc.)	$0.20	$0.15	$0.10	S
Hoyle Double Deck Sets in Plastic Cases, Various Designs	$5.00	$4.00	$2.50	DD
Jumbo Decks, up to 8 inches in length	$5.00	$4.00	$2.50	J
Kem Brand, Double Deck Sets in Marked Cases, 1950s–1970s	$8.00	$6.00	$4.00	DD
Local Advertising	$0.20	$0.15	$0.10	S
Mini-Decks, 2 1/4" x 1 1/2"	$3.00	$2.00	$1.50	M
NASCAR	$8.00	$6.00	$4.00	S
Oil/Gas Companies	$6.00	$4.50	$3.00	S
Pin-Up Girls, Modern, 1970s—Up (aka Adult, Gaiety, Nude Models)	$5.00	$4.00	$2.50	S
Pin-Up Girls, Older, 1950s–1960s	$12.00	$9.00	$6.00	S
Pin-Up Girls, Antique, 1940s & Before	$20.00	$15.00	$10.00	S
Piatnik Austria/European 2-Deck Sets with Fancy Cards	$12.00	$9.00	$6.00	DD
Railroads, Late 1890s/Early 1900s, Leather Case	$100.00	$75.00	$50.00	S
Railroads—Large Trains or Train Engines	$30.00	$22.50	$15.00	S
Railroads—Lettering Only	$10.00	$7.50	$5.00	S
Round Decks	$5.00	$4.00	$2.50	R
Soft Drinks, Modern, 1970s—Up	$6.00	$4.50	$3.00	S
Soft Drinks with Models or Pin-Ups Girls, 1950s and 1960s	$15.00	$11.50	$7.50	S
Sports, Pro Teams	$6.00	$4.50	$3.00	S
Stancraft, Double Deck Sets in Plastic Cases, 1950s–1970s	$8.00	$6.00	$4.00	DD
Tins, Decorative Double Deck Sets in Tins	$10.00	$7.50	$5.00	DD
Tiny Decks (smaller than mini's)	$2.00	$1.50	$1.00	T
Tourist/Souvenir, Antique (75 years or older)			$50.00	S
Tourist/Souvenir, Modern	$4.00	$3.00	$2.00	S
Tourist/Souvenir, Single Decks in Tin	$6.00	$4.50	$3.00	S
Whiskey or Whisky (English Spelling "Whisky")	$8.00	$6.00	$4.00	S

$100 Bill, Canada. $2.00

$100 Bill, U.S. Front. $2.00

$100 Bill, U.S. Rear. $2.00

101 Dalmatians. $5.00

3M CS2 TelComm. $2.00

A Class Brand. $1.00

AAA #99 Brand, Red. $1.00

AAA #99 Brand, Blue. $1.00

AAA Brand, Blue. $1.00

AAA Brand, Pink. $1.00

AAA China Gold Brand. $1.50

Absolut Vodka. $6.00

Aces over Kings Brand Blue. $2.00

Aces over Kings Brand Red. $2.00

Acme Fast Freight. $3.00

Adobe Acrobat. $4.50

Adventureland. $2.00

Air France. $6.00

Air Jamaica. $6.00

Aircraft Spotter, 1979. $9.00

Airplane Spotter, 1943. $50.00

Aladdin Hotel & Casino. $1.50

Alaska Railroad in Tin. $9.00

Alaska Bush Plane Tourist. $1.50

Alaska-Seattle Cruise Line. $4.00

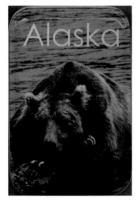

Alaska, Bear in Tin. $4.50

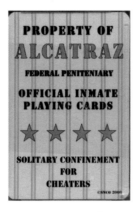

Alcatraz Prison. $3.00

Alcatraz Prison (2). $3.00

AMC Pacer. $6.00

American Airlines DH4 Biplane.
$10.00

American Airlines, AA in Squares.
$4.00

American Airlines, Eagle with AA.
$4.00

American Airlines, Eagle in Circle.
$4.00

American Airlines, Lettering. $4.00

American Airlines, Rows of A's. $4.00

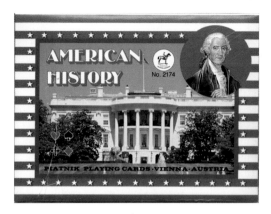

American History. $15.00

American Iron & Machine Works. $3.00

American Yacht Club. $3.00

American Eagle. $5.00

Amma Military, 1941. $75.00

Amtrak, Blue Border. $4.50

Amtrak, Red Border. $4.50

Angel Fire Resort. $1.50

Animal Kingdom, Disney. $3.00

Ante by Umbra. $6.00

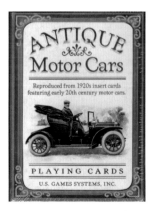

Antique Motor Cars. $5.00

Apollo Brand, 1890. $75.00

Apple Barn. $1.50

Aristocrat Brand. $1.00

Arizona Souvenir. $1.00

Arizona Tourist Parks. $1.50

Arizona Tourist, Sedona. $1.50

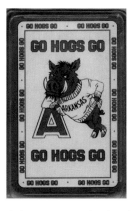

Arkansas Razorbacks. $4.00

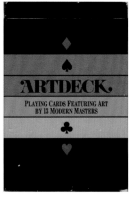

Art Deck by Piatnik. $6.00

Art Deck by Piatnik, Bridgeman Library, Monet Backs. $6.00

Art Deck by Piatnik, The Nude. $6.00

Art Deck, Oriental, Dream of Red Mansions. $6.00

Atlanta Olympics. $4.00

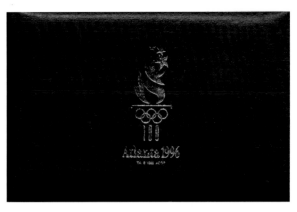

Atlanta Olympics, Two-Deck Set. $11.00

Atlantic City. $3.00

Atlantic City with gambling icons. 1970s

Atlantis Casino. $1.50

Atomic Fireball. $6.00

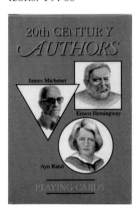

Authors. $4.00

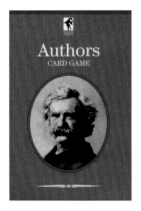

Authors, 20th Century. $4.00

Authors, Classic. $4.00

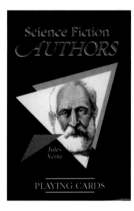

Authors, Science Fiction. $4.00

Aviator Brand. $1.50

Aviator Blue Stamp Seal, 1949. $2.00

Bacardi Summer of Rum. $5.00

Barton Brand. $1.00

Baseball Mini Deck. $1.50

Basic Cigarettes. $4.50

Basic Cigarettes. $6.00

Basketball Mini Deck. $1.50

Batman Animated Cartoon. $6.00

Batman Animated Cartoon (2). $6.00

Batman Movie, Jack Nicholson Joker. $17.50

Batman, Bat Logo. $9.00

Batman Begins. $5.00

Batman Mini. $4.00

Batman Returns. $5.00

Beatles. $16.00

Bee Brand #92, 1950s. $3.00

Bee Brand, Jumbo Index. $1.50

Bee Club Special Cambric Finish
Jumbo Index. $2.00

Belle of Louisville. $6.00

Ben & Jerry's Ice Cream. $5.00

Benson & Hedges Cigarettes, Gray
Pack. $4.50

Benson & Hedges Cigarettes, Tan
Pack 1. $4.50

Benson & Hedges Cigarettes, Tan
Pack 2. $4.50

Benson & Hedges. $6.00

Betty Boop. $7.50

BF Goodrich. $3.00

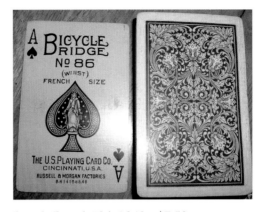

Bicycle Brand #86, 1920s. $10.00

Bicycle Brand #86, 1940s. $7.50

Bicycle Brand #808, 1895. $85.00

Bicycle Brand #808, 1920s. $75.00

Bicycle Brand #808, Acorn Backs. $7.50

Bicycle Brand #8082, Jumbo. $9.00

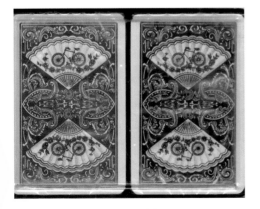

Bicycle Brand, Bicycles. $6.00

Bicycle Brand, Jumbo Size, 7.5 x 4.5. $9.00

Bicycle Brand, Mini. $2.00

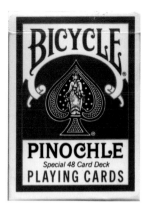

Bicycle Brand, Pinochle. $1.00

Bicycle Brand, Red Canasta, 1960s. $7.50

Bicycle Rider Backs in Tin. $9.00

Bicycle Rider Backs Red. $1.00

Bicycle Rider Backs, Blue. $1.00

Bicycle Rider Back.

Bicycle Tall Stacks, 1980s. $4.00

Bicycle 125th Anniversary, 2010. $2.00

Bicycle Clear. $3.00

Bicycle Modern Jumbo Index. $2.00

Bicycle War Bonds. $40.00

Bicycle#86 Blue, 1956. $10.00

Bicycle#86 Red, 1956. $10.00

Bicycle Brand B & W. $3.00

Bicycle Brand Black & Gray. $3.00

Bicycle Rider Back 4 Bicycle 010. $3.00

Big Ben. $3.00

Big Boy. $6.00

Binions Casino. $1.50

Biscuits by Piatnik. $9.00

Bit-O-Honey. $9.00

Black & White Whiskey. $7.50

Black Velvet Whiskey. $7.50

Black Velvet Whiskey (2). $7.50

Blatz Beer Can Shape. $10.00

Blue Bonnet. $7.50

Blue Cross Blue Shield. $3.00

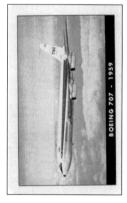

Boeing 707. $10.00

Boeing 727. $10.00

Boeing 747. $10.00

Boeing Stratoliner. $10.00

Boheme Cruise Lines. $4.50

Bohemia Moravia by Piatnik. $9.00

Boomtown Casino. $1.50

Boomtown Wild West Casino. $1.50

Border Collies & Sheep. $1.00

Botticelli by Piatnik. $9.00

Botticelli Piatnik. $12.00 Mint in Box (MIB)

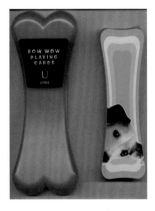

Bow Wow Bones. $6.00

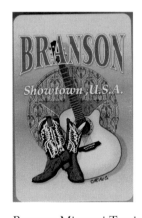

Branson Missouri Tourist. (1) $4.00

Branson Missouri Tourist. (2) $4.00

Branson Missouri Tourist. (3) $4.00

Branson. $3.00

Bridge Brand. $1.00

Bronners. $3.00

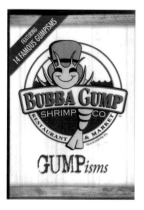

Bubba Gumpisms. $5.00

Buckingham Palace, London. $2.00

Bucks Brand. $1.00

Bucks Brand. $1.50 MIB

Bucks Brand Red. $1.50

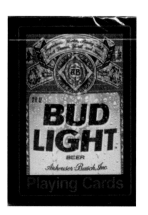

Bud Light. $4.50

Bud Light (2). $4.50

Bud Light. $6.00

Budweiser 24 Pack. $6.00

Budweiser Girl. $12.50

Budweiser Girl (2). $12.50

Budweiser House. $6.00

Budweiser King of Beers. $4.50

Budweiser Lizards. $6.00

Budweiser Logo. $6.00

Budweiser Logo (2). $6.00

Budweiser Bottle Label. $6.00

Bugs Bunny. $6.00

Bulldog Squeezers Back. $2.00

Bulldog Squeezers Front. $2.00

Bush George W Deck. $5.00

Buster Brown Cards, 1906. $75.00

Buster Brown, 1906. $75.00

Cabelas. $3.00

Cabinet Brand, 1890. $150.00

Caesars Palace. $1.50

Caesars Palace, Blue Deck. $1.50

Caesars Palace, Red Deck. $1.50

California Baccarat Casino. $1.50

California Hotel & Casino. $1.50

California Poppy, Reider, 1911. $75.00

California Souvenir Early Twentieth Century.
$50.00

Calvert Brands. $4.50

Camel Pack Design. $6.00

Camel Pack Design (2). $6.00

Camel Pack Design (3). $6.00

Camel, 23 Small Camels. $4.50

Camel, Joe Camel. $4.50

Camel, Joe Camel (2). $4.50

Camel, Joe Camel (3). $4.50

Camel Joe Camel (4). $6.00

Camp Snoopy. $4.50

Campbell's Alphabet Set. $15.00

Campbell's Chunky Soup. $6.00

Canada Flag. $3.00

Canada Flag, Mini Deck. $2.00

Canadian Club. $4.50

Capital Airlines. $3.00

Captain Morgan. $6.00

Care Bears. $4.50

Caribbean Cruise Lines. $4.50

Carling Black Label Can Shape.
$10.00

Carnival, New Orleans, 1926. $50.00

Carnival, Large Cruise Ship. $4.00

Carnival, Mardi Gras Ship. $4.50

Carnival Cruise, Mardi Gras. $6.00

Carnivale, Madi Gras Lettering. $4.00

Carolans Irish Cream. $6.00

Casa Loma. $3.00

Casablanca Rick's Cafe, Double Set. $12.00

Casablanca, Rick's Cafe, 2004 Reissue. $9.00

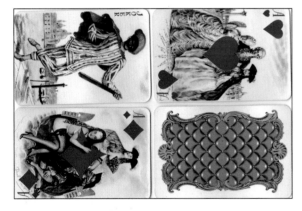

Casanova Becat. $300.00

Casanova Becat, French Nudes. $300.00

Casino Royale, James Bond DD, 2007. $10.00

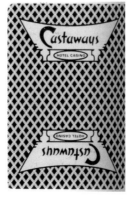

Castaways Casino, Blue Deck. $1.50

Castaways Casino, Red Deck. $1.50

51

Castle Rock. $3.00

Cat & Ball Brand. $1.50

Caterpillar Equipment. $6.00

Cavalier Cigarettes. $4.50

Cedar Point. $3.00

Centennial Olympics. $4.50

Century of Progress, Chicago, 1933.
$30.00

Champion Brand. $1.50

Champion Brand. $2.00

Champion, Globes. $4.00

Cheetos. $4.50

Cheetos (2). $4.50

Chevrolet Erotosi. $4.50

Chevrolet, 1962. $6.00

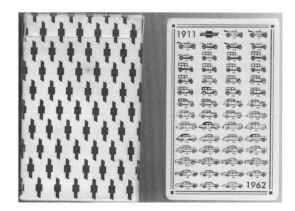

Chevrolet Tin Set. $7.50

Chicago Bulls. $6.00

Chicago Tourist. $3.00

Chicago Tourist Icons. $3.00

Chicago World's Fair, 1934. $30.00

China Brand. $0.75

China Shanghai Hotel. $1.00

Chinese Folk Customs Souvenir. $4.00

Chinese Historical Spots Souvenir. $4.00

Chinese Mao Tourist. $4.00

Chinese Shanghai Museum Souvenir. $4.00

Chinese Terra Cotta Soldiers Souvenir. $4.00

Chinese Tiny Deck, 1" x 1 1/2". $0.50

Chinese Xian Souvenir. $4.00

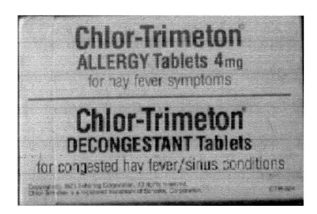

Chlor-Trimeton. $3.00

Christmas Cards. $6.00

Christmas Carol Dickens Double Set. $6.00

Christmas Holiday Green. $2.00

Christmas Holiday Red. $2.00

Christmas Snowman 2006. $3.00

Christmas Story. $9.00

Christmas Tree 2006. $3.00

Chunky Soup. $6.00

Cigar Poker by Piatnik. $4.50

Cincinnati Reds, Tiny Deck. $3.00

Cincinnati Zoo. $3.00

Cinderella Mini. $3.00

Circus Circus Casino. $1.50

Citgo. $6.00

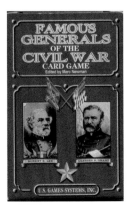

Civil War Generals. $4.00

Civil War Union Generals. $4.00

Clifden, Ireland. $4.00

Club Cal Casino. $1.50

CN Railroad. $15.00

Coca Cola (1). $4.50

Coca Cola (2). $4.50

Coca Cola (3). $4.50

Coca Cola (4). $4.50

Coca Cola (5). $4.50

Coca Cola (6). $4.50

Coca Cola (7). $4.50

Coca Cola Advertising, 1943. $100.00

Coca Cola Fly Girl, WWII. $75.00

Coca Cola, Tin Set. $9.00

Coca Cola 1994 Set in Tin. $12.00

Coca Cola 2008 DS. $10.00

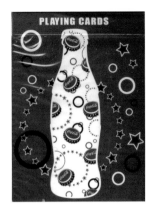

Coca Cola Bottle & Stars. $6.00

Coca Cola Good Taste. $6.00

Coca Cola Lady at Table. $6.00

Coca Cola Rockwell Christmas. $6.00

Columbian Exposition, 1893. $150.00

Combat Vehicle ID, 1985. $7.50

Compagnie Cruise Lines. $4.00

Confederate Flag. $4.00

Congress Minnehaha, 1947. $30.00

Congress 606 Barn 1920s. $20.00

Congress 606 Barn Ace of Spades. $20.00

Congress 606 Joker. $9.00

Congress 606 Box Front, Barn, 1930. $20.00

Congress 606 Pinochle Leather Case, 1930s. $12.00

Congress Brand, 1870s. $75.00

Congress Brand, 1950s Hogier. $4.00

Congress Brand, 1960s. $4.00

Congress CelUTone Finish, 1950s. $4.00

Conoco. $4.50

Consolidated Pinochle, 1885. $25.00

Contac. $7.50

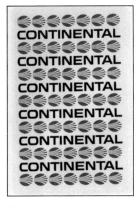

Continental Airlines, Alternating Rows. $4.00

Continental Airlines, Circle Logo. $4.00

Continental Airlines, Lettering. $4.00

Cool Whip. $6.00

Coors Beer, Lettering. $4.50

Coors Light. $6.00

Coors Logo. $6.00

Coors Logo (2). $6.00

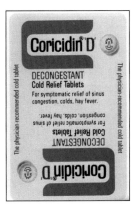

Coricidin. $4.50

Country Music, Best of. $6.00

Country Music Hall of Fame. $3.00

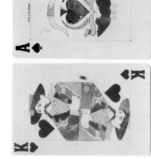

Cowboys. $3.00

Cracker Barrel. $6.00

Cracker Jack. $6.00

Crayola Crayons. $6.00

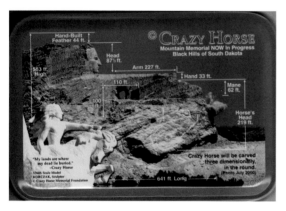

Crazy Horse Tin. $4.00

Cream of Wheat. $8.00

Credit Union. $1.50

Crocodile Hunter. $4.50

Crooked Deck Backs. $4.50

Crooked Deck Box. $4.50

Crooked Wide Deck. $6.00

Crown Brand. $6.00

Crown Royal. $6.00

Cutty Sark Scots Whisky. $12.00

CVS Brand. $1.50

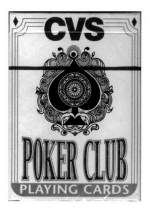

CVS Poker Club Brand. $2.00

Da Vinci. $6.00

Dallas Cowboys. $6.00

Delta Air Lines Globe. $5.00

Delta Air Lines New Orleans. $4.00

Delta Air Lines, Miami, City. $7.50

Delta Air Lines, Atlanta, City. $7.50

Delta Air Lines, Atlanta, Lady. $7.50

Delta Air Lines, Bermuda. $7.50

Delta Air Lines, Boston. $7.50

Delta Air Lines, Chicago, City. $7.50

Delta Air Lines, Chicago, Man. $7.50

Delta Air Lines, Detroit. $7.50

Delta Air Lines, Florida. $7.50

Delta Air Lines, Houston, City. $7.50

Delta Air Lines, Houston, Oil Worker. $7.50

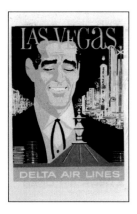

Delta Air Lines, Las Vegas. $10.00

Delta Air Lines, Lines. $4.00

Delta Air Lines, Los Angeles. $10.00

Delta Air Lines, Los Angeles, Cleopatra & Bobby. $7.50

Delta Air Lines, Miami. $7.50

Delta Air Lines, Miami & Fort Lauderdale. $7.50

Delta Air Lines, New England. $7.50

Delta Air Lines, New Orleans City. $7.50

Delta Air Lines, New Orleans Jazz. $7.50

Delta Air Lines, New York City. $7.50

Delta Air Lines, New York Cop. $7.50

Delta Air Lines, New York, Statue of Liberty. $7.50

Delta Air Lines, Puerto Rico. $7.50

Delta Air Lines, San Francisco Street Car. $7.50

Delta Air Lines, San Francisco, Oriental. $7.50

Delta Air Lines, Washington, DC, Jefferson Memorial. $7.50

Delta Line Cruise Ship. $4.50

Delta Air Lines. $4.00

Delta Airlines Chicago. $7.50

Delta Airlines Dallas/Fort Worth. $7.50

Delta Air Lines, Las Vegas. $7.50

Delta Air Lines, Los Angeles. $7.50

Desert Inn Casino. $1.50

Desert Inn Casino, Red Deck. $1.50

Desert Inn Casino, White Deck. $1.50

Detroit Lions. $4.50

Detroit Red Wings. $4.50

Detroit Red Wings (2). $4.50

Detroit Tigers. $4.50

Detroit Tigers, 2008. $6.00

Detroit Tigers, 2009. $6.00

Detroit Tigers Hero Deck. $5.00

Dial Soap. $8.00

Dinosaurs, The Age of. $5.00

Discovery Channel. $4.50

Disney Princesses. $4.50

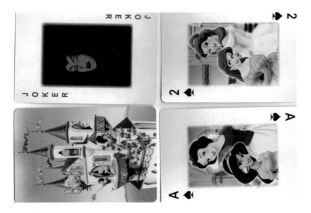

Disney Princesses. $6.00

Disney World, Cinderella Castle. $4.00

Disneyland, Cinderella Castle. $4.00

Disneyland, Mini. $2.00

Disneyland, Mini (2). $2.00

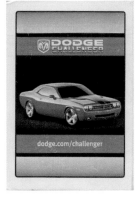

Dodge Challenger. $6.00

Dogs Playing Poker, Tin Set. $7.50

Dolly Parton. $5.00

Dominos Pizza, Box. $4.00

Dominos Pizza, Noid. $4.00

Dondorf #174, Swiss, 1906. $100.00

Donkey Kong Junior. $6.00

Doritos. $4.50

Dorney Park. $3.00

Dougherty, 1850s. $250.00

Dougherty Pinochle. $25.00

Douglas DC-3. $12.00

Douglas, DC-4. $12.00

Douglas, DC-9. $12.00

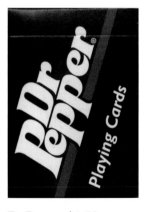

Dr Pepper. $4.50

Dr. Van Dyke's Holland Bitters. $150.00

Dracula Creepy Classics. $5.00

Drueke. $6.00

DuPont. $3.00

Duncan Hines Cake Mix, 1951. $16.00

Dunkin' Donuts. $7.50

Duo-Fast Tools. $1.00

Duracell. $6.00

Durango & Silverton. $7.50

Duratone Set. $6.00

Early Times. $6.00

Easter Bunny in Tin. $4.50

Easter Egg in Tin. $4.00

Eastern Airlines. $4.00

Eastern Steamship Lines. $4.50

Eastern State Penitentiary. $2.00

Eckerd Brand. $2.00

Edgewater Hotel and Casino. $2.00

Edward Scissorhands in Tin. $6.00

Egypt Tourist 2008. $4.00

Eight Hundred Eighteen Poker
Brand. $2.00

Eight Ball Round Deck. $6.00

El Cortez Casino, Blue Deck. $1.50

El Cortez Casino, Red Deck. $1.50

El Mirador Hotel. $4.00

Elsie the Cow. $7.50

Elvis (1). $7.50

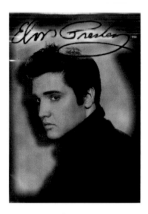

Elvis (2). $7.50

Elvis, Best Of. $9.00

Epcot Center. $3.00

Epcot Center (2). $3.00

ESPN The Magazine. $2.00

Europe. $3.00

Evinrude, Family. $7.50

Evinrude, Man on Boat. $6.00

Evinrude, Outboard Motors. $4.50

Exportation, Brand, Original Deck.
$150.00

Exportation, Reproduction Deck.
$6.00

Falstaff Beer, 1940s. $15.00

Farrell Cruise Lines. $4.50

Felix the Cat. $4.50

Fifty & Over Set. $4.50

Firestone, the People Tire. $7.50

Fitzgeralds Casino. $1.50

Fitzgeralds Casino, Blue Deck. $1.50

Fitzgeralds Casino, Red Deck. $1.50

Five Sixty Two Brand. $3.00

Five Sixty Two Brand, Reverse. $3.00

Flag Brand Giant Face. $1.50

Flag Brand Poker. $1.50

Flamingo Capri Hotel & Casino. $1.50

Flamingo Capri Hotel & Casino, Blue Deck. $1.50

Fleischmann's Gin. $6.00

Fleischmann's Multi-Brand. $6.00

Florida, Early 20th Century. $50.00

Fluid King. $1.50

Flying Eagle 280 Brand. $2.00

Football Mini Deck. $2.00

Ford GT, 1950s. $10.00

Ford Motor Company. $4.50

Ford Motor Company. $4.50

Ford Motor Company (2). $4.50

Ford Tri-Motor. $12.00

Ford, Tin Set. $7.50

Fort Howard Paper. $1.50

Fortune Deck 1896. $50.00

Fortune Deck (2) 1896. $50.00

Four Queens Casino. $1.50

Four Queens Casino, Blue Deck. $1.50

Four Queens Casino, Red Deck. $1.50

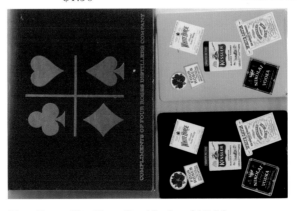

Four Roses Distillery Double Set. $12.00

Fox Lake Brand. $1.00

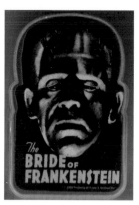

Frankenstein, The Bride of, Creepy Classics. $5.00

Fred Olsen Cruise Lines. $4.50

Fremont Hotel & Casino. $1.50

Fremont Hotel & Casino (2). $1.50

Fritos. $4.50

Frontier Hotel & Casino. $1.50

Game of Flags, French, 1880s. $250.00

Gander Mountain. $4.50

Garfield (1). $4.00

Garfield (2). $4.00

Garfield Tin Set. $9.00

Gatorade, Green Deck. $4.50

Gatorade Orange Deck. $4.50

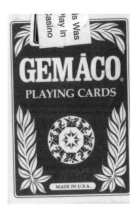

Gemaco Brand. $1.00

General Jackson Cruise Ship. $3.00

General Motors. $3.00

General Motors (2). $3.00

Gerber Baby Formula. $6.00

Gerber Set. $12.00

G.I. Joe Set in Tin. $7.50

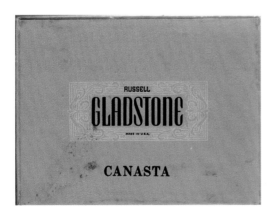

Gladstone Brand by Russell, 1950s. $2.00

Godzilla, King of the Lizards, Creepy
Classics. $5.00

Gold Spike Casino, Blue Deck. $1.50

Gold Spike Casino, Red Deck. $1.50

Golden Class Brand. $1.50

Golden Gate Bridge, San Francisco. $3.00

Golden Gate Casino, Blue Deck. $1.50

Golden Gate Casino, Red Deck. $1.50

Golden Nugget Casino, Black Deck. $1.50

Golden Nugget Casino, Black Gambling Hall. $1.50

Golden Nugget Casino, Blue Deck. $1.50

Golden Nugget Casino, Red Deck. $1.50

Golden Nugget Casino, Sign. $1.50

Golden Nugget Casino, Green Gambling Hall. $2.00

Golden Nugget Casino, Red Gambling Hall. $1.50

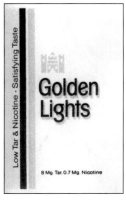

Golden Lights Cigarettes. $4.50

Golden Lights Cigarettes. $6.00

Golden Lights Cigarettes (2). $6.00

Goodyear. $3.00

Goodrich Silvertowns. $3.00

Graceland. $3.00

Grand Canyon. $3.00

Grand Hotel Mini Deck, Mackinac Island, Michigan. $2.00

Grand Hotel. $3.00

Grand Hotel, Mackinac Island, Michigan 2008. $4.00

Grand Ole Opry House. $3.00

Grand Ole Opry, Nashville, Tenn.
$3.00

Grateful Dead. $8.00

Grateful Dead, 1998. $7.50

Great Lakes Lighthouses. $3.00

Great Lakes Ships. $3.00

Great Smoky Mountains, Bear, 2010.
$1.00

Greektown Casino. $1.50

Guinness Beer. $6.00

Gulf Indy 500. $4.50

Gulf Research Center.
$4.50

Gypsy Witch. $30.00

Hacienda Casino. $1.50

Halloween 1 2006. $2.00

Halloween 2 2006. $2.00

Halloween 3 2006. $2.00

Hamm's Beer, River Scene. $7.50

Handy Helpful Hints. $2.00

Happy Bunny. $4.50

Happy Chef. $2.00

Hard Rock Casino. $1.50

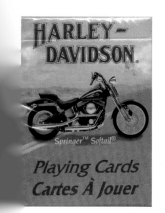

Harley Davidson (1). $4.50

Harley Davidson (2). $4.50

Harley Davidson (3). $4.50

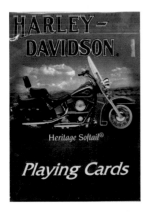

Harley Davidson (4). $4.50

Harley Davidson (5). $4.50

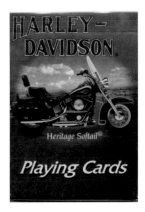

Harley Davidson (6). $4.50

Harley Davidson Tin Set (1). $9.00

Harley Davidson Tin Set (2). $9.00

Harley Davidson Cigarettes. $6.00

Harolds Club Casino, Black Deck.
$1.50

Harolds Club Casino, Red Deck.
$1.50

Harrah's Casino. $1.50

Hawaii (1). $3.00

Hawaii (2). $3.00

Heart Shaped. $2.00

Hell, MI. $3.00

Hello Kitty. $6.00

Henry Ford Museum. $3.00

Hershey Chefs' Set. $7.50

Hershey's Mini Deck. $2.00

Hershey's Syrup. $11.50

Hershey's Syrup. $15.00 MIB

Hertz Rent-a-Car Set. $7.50

Hickory Farms. $8.00

Highlanders Brand, 1864. $350.00

Hilton Hotel & Casino, Blue Deck. $1.50

Hilton Hotel & Casino, Red Deck. $1.50

Hispania by Piatnik. $9.00

Holiday Casino, Blue Deck. $1.50

Holiday Casino, Red Deck. $1.50

Holiday Inn Sign. $7.50

Holland American Cruise Lines, Boat in Oval. $4.50

Holland American Cruise Lines, Ship. $4.50

Honda Motorcycles 1970s. $6.00

Hong Kong Bridge & Castle. $4.00

Honk Kong Round Cards. $4.50

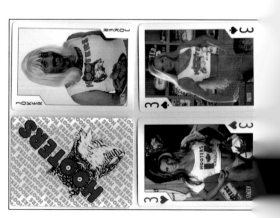

Hooters 1997. $10.00

Horseshoe Club Casino. $1.50

Hot Springs National Park. $3.00

Hot Wheels (1). $4.50

Hot Wheels (2). $4.50

Hot Wheels, Tin Set. $9.00

Hot Wheels (3). $4.50

Hotpoint All Electric Kitchen, 1950s. $6.00

Hovis Bread, 1890s. $100.00

Hoyle Brand Pinochle. $1.00

Hoyle Brand Examples, Pinochle and Standard. $1.00 Each

Hoyle Brand. $1.00

Hoyle Double Deck Set. $4.00

Hulk, 2003. $4.00

Hustling Joe Transformation, 1895.
$750.00

IBM Quarter Century Club.
$1.00

Ice Capades, 1960s. $6.00

Illinois State Outline. $1.00

Illusions Set. $7.50

Imperial Brand. $2.00

Inca, 1948. $50.00

Inca Dynasty Peru Tourist. $2.00

Incredible Hulk. $4.50

Incredibles, The. $4.50

Independence Hall. $1.00

Indiana Jones DD. $10.00

Indianapolis 500. $6.00

Instant Cash. $1.00

Intel Fax Modem. $4.50

Inter-Mountain, 1920s. $50.00

Invincible Pinochle 303 Brand. $4.00

Iowa Mini Deck. $2.00

Ireland, Find. $1.00

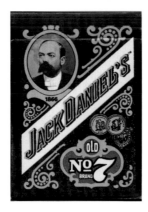

Jack Daniel's (1). $6.00

Jack Daniel's (2). $6.00

Jack Daniel's (3). $6.00

Jack Daniel's Gentleman's. $8.00

Jack Daniel's Old No. 7. $8.00

Jaeger Equipment. $6.00

James Bond, 40th Anniversary Set.
$12.00

Jameson Irish Whiskey. $8.00

Jefferson Standard Life Insurance.
$3.00

Jerry's Nugget Casino, Black Deck.
$1.50

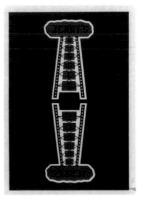

Jerry's Nugget Casino, Blue Deck.
$1.50

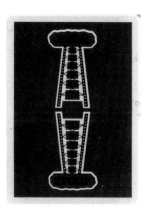

Jerry's Nugget Casino, Red Deck.
$1.50

Jerry's Nugget Casino, Red Deck (2).
$1.50

Jim Beam (1). $6.00

Jim Beam (2). $6.00

Joe's Crab Shack. $4

John Ascuaga's Nugget Casino, Black
Deck. $1.50

John Ascuaga's Nugget Casino, Red
Deck. $1.50

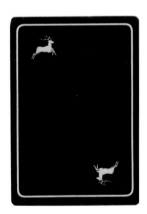

John Deere Logo (1). $4.50

John Deere Logo (2). $4.50

John Deere, Nothing Runs Like a
Deere. $6.00

Johnnie Walker Black Label. $6.00

Johnnie Walker Red. $4.50

Joy Tyme Brand. $3.00

Judge Brand Pinochle, 1950s. $4.50

Jumbo Red. $2.00

Jumbo Red, French. $2.00

Jurassic Park. $9.00

Kaiser by Piatnik. $9.00

Kansas City Southern Lines' Set. $12.00

Kay Jewelers' Set. $4.50

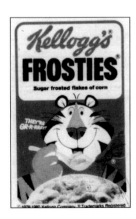

Kellogg's Frosties. $6.00

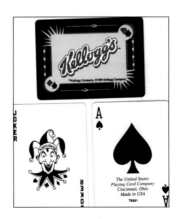

Kellogg's 1994. $4.00

Kem Leaf Backs, 1935. $30.00

Kenmore Washer, 1960s. $4.50

Kennedy Kards. $40.00 MIB

Kennedy Kards, 1963. $30.00

Kent Cigarettes (1). $4.50

Kent Cigarettes (2). $4.50

Kent Cigarettes, Chess Pieces. $6.00

Kentucky Fried Chicken. $12.00

Killark Electric. $1.00

King Kong, Creepy Classics. $5.00

Kings Island. $3.00

Kingsir Brand, China. $1.00

KisMe Cooks. $2.00

Knights of Camelot Set. $12.00

Knott's Berry Farm. $3.00

Knott's Berry Farm (2). $3.00

Kool Cigarettes, Kool & Mild Today.
$6.00

Kool Cigarettes, Milds. $6.00

Kool Cigarettes, Milds. $6.00

Kool-Aid. $7.50

Korean Airlines. $4.00

L & M Oilfield. $4.50

L & N Block Scenes. $7.50

La Cage. $2.00

Lady by Piatnik. $9.00

Las Vegas. $3.00

Las Vegas Club Casino, Black Deck.
$1.50

Las Vegas Club Casino, Red Deck.
$1.50

Las Vegas 100th Anniversary Set.
$6.00

Las Vegas Tourist (1). $2.00

Las Vegas Tourist (2). $2.00

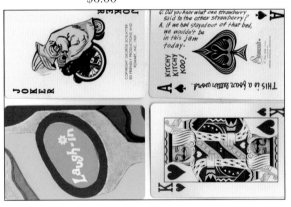

Laugh-In, 1969. $10.00

Lays. $4.50

LBJ, The Texas White House. $3.00

Lenox Tools. $3.00

Lewis & Clark, 200th Anniversary, 2004. $3.00

Life Savers. $7.50

Lincoln National Life Insurance. $4.50

Lisa Frank. $3.00

Lite Beer Logo. $6.00

Lite Beer, Lettering. $4.50

Little Dukes. $8.00

Lockheed 749, 1950. $16.00

Lockheed 1049, 1952. $16.00

Lockheed 1049G, 1955. $16.00

Lockheed 1649, 1957. $16.00

London Guard in Tin. $4.50

Lone Star Beer. $6.00

Looney Tunes, 4 Squares. $6.00

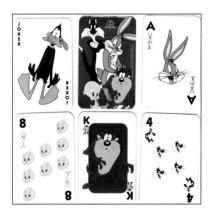

Looney Tunes Mini. $4.00

Los Angeles Olympics, 1984. $4.00

Louis XV, Grimaud, France, 1890. $125.00

Love Boat Cruise. $4.00

Love Stamp, USPS. $4.50

Lummi Casino. $1.50

Luxury by Pilatnik. $9.00

Michigan State Police. $4.00

M&Ms. $6.00

M&Ms. $8.00

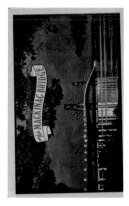

Mackinac Bridge. $3.00

Mackinac Bridge Mini. $1.00

Mackinac Island. $3.00

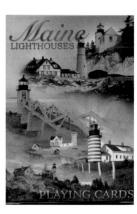

Maine Lighthouses. $3.00

Malaysia, Dolphin Brand, Black Deck. $0.75

Malaysia, Dolphin Brand, Red Deck. $0.75

Mallard Ducks' Set by Kem. $10.50

Mammoth Cave. $3.00

Manchester Liners. $4.50

Mao Chinese. $6.00

Marathon, The Ohio Company. $3.00

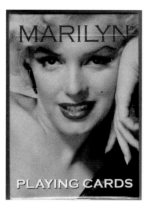

Marilyn Monroe New (1). $6.00

Marilyn Monroe New (2). $6.00

Marlboro Cigarettes. $4.50

Marlboro Man. $6.00

Marlboro Man, Double Deck Set. $15.00

Martin 404, 1950. $12.00

Mash 4077th. $7.50

Maverick Brand, Pinochle. $1.00

Maverick Brand, Revolver, 1940s. $15.00

Maxine, Double Deck Hallmark Set. $6.00

McDonald's. $12.00

Merit Cigarettes. $4.50

Merit Cigarettes. $6.00

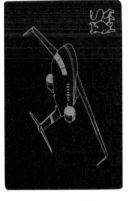

Merryl Lynch. $4.50

MGM Grand Casino, Blue Deck.
$1.50

MGM Grand Casino, Red Deck.
$1.50

MGM Grand, Red. $2.00

MGS Brand. $1.50

Michelin, Repeated Tire Pattern.
$6.00

Michelob Beer Logo (1). $6.00

Michelob Beer Logo (2). $6.00

Michigan Lighthouses. $3.00

Michigan Lottery. $1.50

Michigan State Tourist. $1.00

Michigan Wolverines. $4.00

Michigan Cherry Festival. $1.00

Michigan Wildflowers. $3.00

Michigan's Upper Peninsula. $3.00

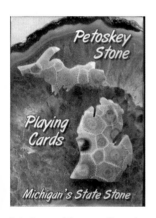

Michigan Tourist, Petoskey Stone.
$1.00

Michigan Tourist, Statehood, 1837.
$1.00

Milwaukee Road Railroad. $4.50

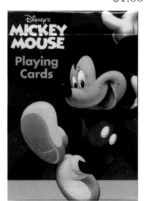

Mickey Mouse, 1990s. $6.00   Mickey Mouse Tin, DD. $12.00

Miller Genuine Draft. $4.50

Miller High Life Logo. $6.00

Miller High Life, Champagne of Beers. $8.00

Miller High Life, Writing. $4.50

Milwaukee Clipper Cruise Ship. $4.50

Minnesota Tourist 2007. $1.00

Mint Hotel & Casino. $1.50

Missouri Double Set. $3.00

MLB Round Deck. $4.50

Mobil Packaging Coatings. $3.00

Mobil Oil Co. $4.00

Monet Lilac Garden by Piatnik. $12.00

Monet Water Lilies by Piatnik. $12.00

Monroe Auto Parts Set. $9.00

Monsters, Inc., Fuzzy Case. $9.00

Montclair WWII. $16.00

Moore McCormick Cruise Lines. $4.50

More Cigarettes. $4.50

Mother's Best Flour 1951. $12.00

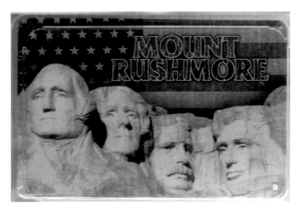

Mount Rushmore, South Dakota. $3.00

Mount Rushmore, 2008. $4.00

Mountain Dew. $4.50

Mountain Dew Action Sports. $6.00

Movie Set, Antique. $80.00

Mr. Potato Head. $9.00

Mummy, Creepy Classics. $5.00

Murphy's Oil Soap. $7.50

Muzak. $3.00

Nabisco Thing. $4.50

Napoleon III 2nd Empire. $5.00

Narragansett Beer. $4.00

NASA, Johnson Space Center. $6.00

Nascar 50th Anniversary. $6.00

Nascar Coca Cola Team. $6.00

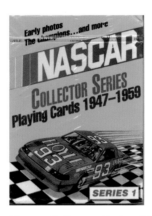

Nascar Collector Series. $6.00

Nascar, Jeff Gordon. $6.00

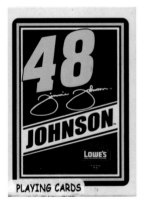

Nascar, Jimmie Johnson. $6.00

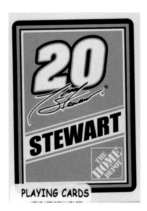

Nascar, Tony Stewart. $6.00

Nashville Zoo. $3.00

National Air & Space Museum (1). $3.00

National Air & Space Museum (2). $3.00

Nation's Capitol, Standing Liberty, 1922. $50.00

Nation's Capital, Sealed. $125.00

Native Americans. $4.50

Naval Warship Spotters, 1970s Issue. $12.00

NCL Cruise Lines. $3.00

Nevada Club Casino. $1.50

New England Mutual Life Insurance. $3.00

New Hampshire, Moose. $3.00

New Hampshire, Tourist Tin. $4.00

New York City Early 20th Century. $50.00

New York Consolidated, 1930s. $20.00

New York New York Casino. $1.50

New York World's Fair Set, 1960s. $9.00

Newport. $6.00

NFL Stars, 1992. $4.50

NFL Tin Set. $7.50

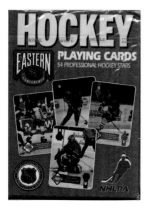

NHL Eastern Stars, 1992. $4.50

NHL Heritage, 1990s. $4.50

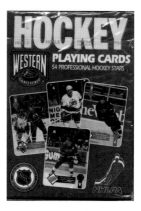

NHL Western Stars, 1992. $4.50

Niagara Falls, Mini Deck. $2.00

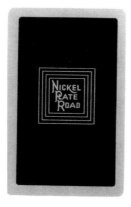

Nickel Plate Railroad, Blue Deck. $6.00

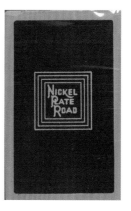

Nickel Plate Railroad, Red Deck. $6.00

Nightmare Before
Christmas. $8.00

Nile Fortune. $50.00

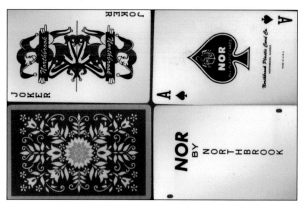

Nor Brand All Plastic 1950s. $3.00

Norman Rockwell, Fall. $4.50

Norman Rockwell, Seasons. $4.50
Each

North Dakota State Outline. $1.00

Northeastern 880 Jets. $4.00

Northwest Airlines, Lettering. $3.00

Norwalk Tire. $3.00

Norway, Norwegian Caribbean Lines,
Lettering. $3.00

Notre Dame University of the 1950s. $6.00

Number 88 Deer Club Brand. $1.00

Number 88 Deer Club Brand, Buck Backs. $1.50

Old Geezer. $3.00

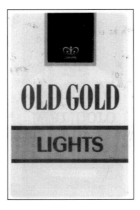

Old Gold Lights Cigarettes. $4.50

Old Milwaukee Beer. $4.50

Old Navy Egg-Shaped Deck. $4.50

Old Style Beer, Bavarian Couple. $4.50

Old Style Beer, Man with Bottle & Glass. $4.50

Old Huckleberry Bourbon. $10.00

Olds is 3rd, Oldsmobile. $4.50

Old Style, Can Shape. $10.00

Old Train, World Famous Arts. $8.00

Omaha Brand. $2.00

Olympia Beer 2 Deck Set. $12.00

One Hundred Pipers Scotch. $4.50

Ostend Dover Cruise Lines. $4.50

Overland Hotel & Casino. $1.50

Ozark Airlines, Black Deck. $4.00

Ozark Airlines, White Deck. $4.00

Ozark Flies Your Way, New Orleans. $6.00

Ozark Flies Your Way, New York. $6.00

Ozark Flies Your Way, San Diego. $8.00

P & O Suit Symbols. $4.00

P & O, Orient Face Card. $4.00

Pacific Far East Line. $4.50

Pacific Northwest. $3.00

Pacific Western Airlines. $4.00

Palace Club Casino. $1.50

Pall Mall Famous Cigarettes. $6.00

Pall Mall Filter Cigarettes (1). $4.50

Pall Mall Filter Tipped Cigarette (2). $4.50

Pan Am, Elephant. $6.00

Pan Am, Large Jet. $6.00

Pan Am, River Scene. $4.00

Pan American, Globe. $4.00

Pan American World Airways,
Winged Globe. $6.00

Panama Canal, 1923. $80.00

Panasonic. $3.00

Paris, Tourist. $4.00

Parthenon, Tennessee. $2.00

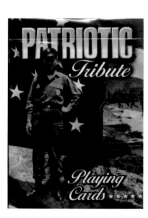

Patriotic Tribute. $4.00

Paulson Brand. $1.50

Paulson Brand, Blue Deck. $1.50

Paulson Brand, Red Deck. $1.50

Peanuts (1). $6.00

Peanuts (2). $6.00

Peanuts (3). $6.00

Peanuts (4). $6.00

Pearl Beer. $6.00

Pearl Light Beer. $6.00

Pella. $3.00

Penn Central Railroad, White
Deck. $4.50

Penn Central Railroad, Black
Deck. $4.50

Penn Mutual Insurance. $3.00

Pennsylvania Railroad, Symbol.
$6.00

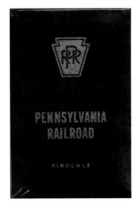

Pennsylvania Railroad, Pinochle
Deck. $7.50

Pennsylvania, Tourist. $3.00

Peoples Brand. $2.00

Pepperidge Farms. $6.00

Pepsi. $4.50

Pepsi (1). $4.50

Pepsi (2). $4.50

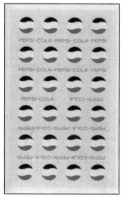

Pepsi (3). $4.50

Pepsi (4). $4.50

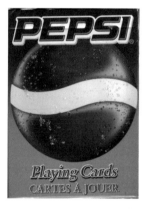

Pepsi, French Version. $6.00

Peter Pan, Miniature. $6.00

Pete's Wicked Winter Brew. $7.50

Philip Morris 100's Cigarettes. $4.50

Phillip Morris, Star Deck in Tin. $6.00

Phoenix Coffee, 1950s. $6.00

Piatnik Birds Mini Double Deck Set, 1950s. $30.00

Piatnik, Tiny Double Deck Set, 1950s. $30.00

Piccadilly Circus, London. $3.00

Piedmont. $4.00

Piedmont. $5.00

Pikes Peak. $3.00

Pillsbury Plus Cake Mix. $7.50

Pin-Up Girls, 1940s. $20.00

Pin-Up Girls, 1950s. $9.00

Pin-Up Girls, 1960s Asian. $12.00

Pin-Up Girls, 1970s. $4.00

Pink Floyd Dark Side of the Moon.
$8.00

Pirate Poker. $4.00

Pirates. $4.00

Pirates of the Caribbean 3. $6.00

Pisa, Leaning Tower. $4.00

Pizza Hut Set. $9.00

Planters Peanuts, 1930.
$50.00

Planters Peanuts, 1930s. $50.00

Playmate 1973 Double Set. $20.00

Plymouth, Mini-Tourist Deck. $2.00

Pokemon 3-Deck Set. $15.00

Polish. $6.00

Politicards, 1971. $15.00

Politicards, 1996. $6.00

Pooh & Friends Mini. $4.00

Porky & Petunia Pig, Looney Tunes, 1990s. $6.00

Power Rangers Mystic Force Die Cut. $4.00

Primadonna Casino. $1.50

Primo Hawaiian Beer. $7.50

Pro Football Hall of Fame. $3.00

Prudential Lines Insurance. $3.00

Qantas Airlines. $4.50

Quest Software. $1.50

Quikrete. $4.50

Rahr Malt. $6.00

Raid. $4.00

Railroads, Multiple Logos. $4.50

Rain Forest Cafe. $6.00

Rainbow Trout, State-O-Maine Brand. $7.50

Raleigh Extra Cigarettes. $6.00

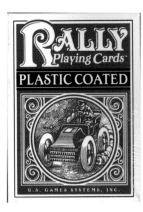

Rally Brand. $2.00

RayOVac Batteries. $4.50

RayOVac Batteries, 1981. $6.00

RC Cola. $4.50

RCA ColorTrak. $3.00

Realtree Hardwoods Camouflage.
$2.00

Red Dog Beer. $7.50

Red Hat Society. $6.00

RediSlip Brand. $2.00

RedNBlue Blue. $1.00

RedNBlue Red. $1.00

Remembrance Brand. $4.00   Remembrance Redi-Slip Brown & Bigelow. $1.00

Reno Tourist. $2.00   Republic Airlines. $3.00   Revco. $3.00

Rexall Brand. $1.00   Rite Aid Drug Store. $2.00   Riviera Casino. $1.50

Riviera Slot World. $2.00   Robert E. Lee Steamboat Set in Tin. $12.00   Robo Car Wash, 1960s. $6.00

Robo Wax Job, 1960s. $6.00

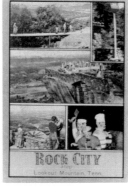

Rock City. $3.00

Rock City (2). $3.00

Rock City, GA. $4.00

Rock Island Railroad. $6.00

Rock Island Route. $75.00

Rockwell International, Astronaut Suits, 1980. $17.50

Rockwell Standard. $3.00

Rococo by Piatnik. $9.00

Rodeo. $2.00

Round Deck. $5.00

Route 66. $4.00

Royal Brand, French. $1.00

Royal Brand, French (2). $1.00

Royal Brand, New York. $1.50 Each

Royal Caribbean Cruise Line (1). $4.50

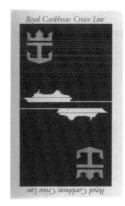

Royal Caribbean Cruise Line (2). $4.50

Rubberset, 1920. $35.00

Ruby Falls Tin. $4.00

Ruilong Brand. $2.00

Rust-Oleum, Green Deck. $6.00

Rust-Oleum, Pink Deck. $6.00

Ruxton Brand. $2.00

Ruxton Brand, 1940. $9.00

S'mores. $4.00

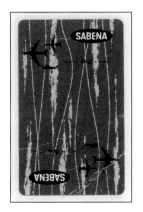

SAE, Double Deck Set. $3.00

Sabena Airlines. $4.00

Sahara Hotel & Casino. $1.50

Sahara Hotel & Casino, Blue Deck. $1.50

Sahara Hotel & Casino, Red Deck. $1.50

Saint Louis Arch. $3.00

Saint Louis, Tourist in Tin. $4.50

Salem Cigarettes (1). $4.50

Salem Cigarettes (2). $4.50

Salem Witch Museum.
$6.00

Samba Triple Set. $4.00

Sands Casino. $1.50

Sands Atlantic City. $2.00

Santa Fe, 2 Trains (1). $30.00

Santa Fe, 2 Trains (2). $30.00

Santa Fe, 2 Trains (3). $30.00

Santa Fe, 1818 Engine. $10.00

Santa Fe, Double Set Engines 5695 & 5696.
$20.00

Santa Fe, 5695 Engine. $10.00

Saturday Evening Post, DD in Tin. $9.00

Saturday Evening Post, Set in Tin. $9.00

Savings of America. $1.00

Scarface (1). $10.00

Scarface (2). $10.00

Schaefer Beer. $3.00

Schlitz Beer, Globe. $6.00

Schlitz Malt Liquor, Bull. $6.00

Schlitz, The Beer that made
Milwaukee Famous. $6.00

Scooby-Doo. $4.50

Scooby-Doo Mini. $3.00

Scooby-Doo Sports. $4.00

Sea World (1). $3.00

Sea World (2). $3.00

Seaboard & Western Airlines. $6.00

Seagram's Gin. $6.00

Seagram's 7 America's Whiskey. $8.00

Seashells. $1.00

Seashore Trolley Museum. $3.00

Seattle Tin. $4.00

Second Empire, French Transformation Deck, 1860. $2,500.00

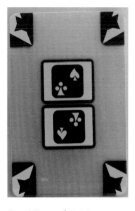

See Thru. $4.00

Seven-Up, The Spot. $7.50

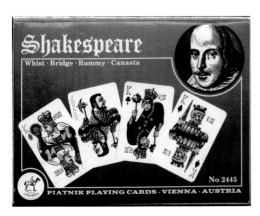

Shakespeare by Piatnik. $9.00

Shamrock by Piatnik. $9.00

Shamrock by Piatnik. $12.00 MIB

Shamrock Hotel. $3.00

Shepherd of the Hills Farm. $3.00

Sherwin Williams. $4.50

Shoebox Greetings, Hallmark, Piatnik Double Deck Set. $6.00

Show World Air Express. $3.00

Silver Art. $6.00

Silver City Casino, Blue Deck. $1.50

Silver City Casino, Red Deck. $1.50

Silver Club Casino, Black Deck. $1.50

Silver Club Casino, Red Deck. $1.50

Silver Nugget Casino. $1.50

Silver Slipper Casino, Black Deck. $1.50

Silver Slipper Casino, Red Deck. $1.50

Simpsons, Bart, 2007. $4.00

Simpsons, Homer, 2007. $4.00

Simpsons Tin. $6.00

Sinclair Oils. $3.00

Six Flags, Texas. $3.00

Skoal Tobacco. $4.00

Slots A Fun Casino. $2.00

Small Soldiers. $6.00

Smiley Face. $4.00

Snap-On Tools. $6.00

Snap On Tools Toolbox. $8.00

Snatch. $8.00

Snirkles. $3.00

Snoopy (1). $6.00

Snoopy (2). $6.00

Soaring Eagle Casino. $1.50

Soaring Eagle Casino. $2.00

Sobelair. $4.00

Society Series, 1890s. $75.00

SOHIO Gas Logo, Eagle. $6.00

Soo Line Railroad, Rural Scene. $22.50

South Dakota Black Hills. $2.00

Southern Comfort Bourbon, Plantation. $7.50

Southern Pacific Lines. $6.00

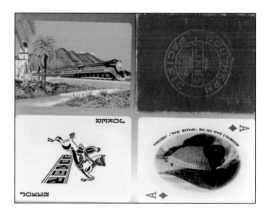

Southern Pacific Lines 1910. $40.00

Southwest Airlines, Coca Cola Promotion, 2004. $3.00

Souvenir Brand. $2.00

Souvenir General. $2.00

Space Shuttle. $4.00

Spider-Man (1), Marvel Comics. $6.00

Spider-Man (2), Marvel Comics. $6.00

Spider-Man (3) Mini 4 Pack. $12.00

Sponge Bob Mini. $4.00

Sponge Bob Nick. $8.00

Sponge Bob Tin DD. $16.00

Sportsman Series. $4.00

Spotters 1984 Armored Vehicle US Army. $12.00

Spotters Replica, 2005. $4.00

Squires London Dry Gin. $4.50

St. Joseph, MO, 1907, Landmarks. $100.00

Stag Beer. $7.50

Stag Party Pack. $12.00

Stage 65X, Cameo Girl, 1908. $125.00

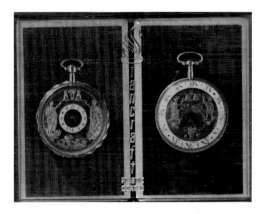

Stancraft Gold Pocket Watch Set. $12.00

Standard Oil. $4.50

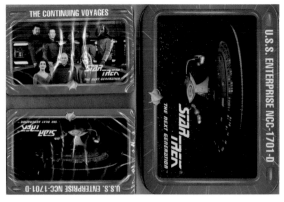

Star Trek Next Generation Tin Set. $12.00

Star Trek, 1960s. $12.00

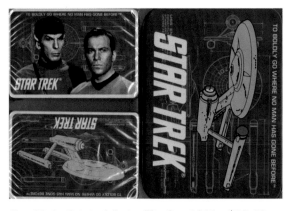

Star Trek, Original Series Tin Set, 1990s. $12.00

Star Wars Episode I, Asian Deck. $6.00

Star Wars Episode I, Canadian Deck. $9.00

Stardust Casino. $2.00

Stardust Hotel & Casino. $1.50

Star Wars Heroes & Villains. $10.00

Star Wars Vehicles. $10.00

Starz Behind Barz. $3.00

States Marine Lines. $4.50

Statue of Liberty. $4.00

Steamboat 999 Black 1955. $12.00

Steamboat 999 Red 1955. $12.00

Stock Index. $2.00

Stratus Brand. $1.50

Streamline No. 1 Brand. $1.50

Streamline Pinochle, U.S. Gov't Issue, 1940s. $4.50

Stroh's Beer. $8.00

Stroh's Beer. $8.00

Stud Brand. $1.50

Sud Americana Cruise Lines. $7.50

Sunoco Gas. $6.00

Sunset Station Casino. $1.50

Survival. $4.00

Swedish American Cruise Lines. $3.00

Sweetnotes. $6.00

Synovate. $1.00

Target. $7.50

Target. $10.00 MIB

Target Stores Suit Symbols. $10.00

TCA Airlines. $4.00

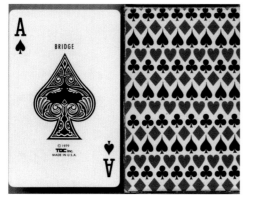

TDC Brand. $1.50

Teenage Mutant Ninja Turtles. $8.00

Teenage Mutant Ninja Turtles, 1980s. $6.00

Tenneco. $2.00

Tennessee Aquarium, Mini Deck. $3.00

Tennessee Aquarium, Mini Deck. $2.00

Tennessee, State Outline. $2.00

Tennessee, Tourist, State Outline. $2.00

Tennessee, University of, DD. $10.00

Texaco Gas Logo. $4.50

Texaco, Worldwide Progress. $4.00

Texas Hold'em. $9.00

Texas Hold'em, Chinese Deck. $2.00

Three-M Company. $3.00

Three-M Company, Building. $3.00

Three-M Company, Plaid. $3.00

Thunderbird Hotel & Casino.
$1.50

Tiny Floral Decks. $1.50 Each

Tommy Hilfiger. $9.00

Tootsie Roll. $8.00

Torpedo Brand, WWII Red Cross
Issue. $9.00

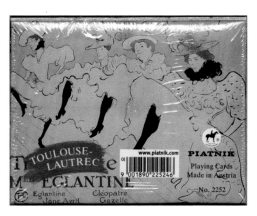

Toulouse Lautrec by Piatnik. $9.00

Townsend Thoresen Cruise Lines. $6.00

Toy Story I. $7.50

Traffic Control Technologies. $0.75

Transformation 19th Century France. $750.00

Transformers. $6.00

Treasure Island Casino. $1.50

Trolls, Morfin. $7.50

Tropicana Casino, Black Deck. $1.50

Tropicana Casino, Blue Deck. $1.50

Trumps Long Cut Pin-up Girls, 1886. $750.00

TT Line Clipper. $3.00

Tuxedo Brand. $1.50 Each

TV Magic Cards, 1970s. $3.00

TWA Lettering in Globe. $4.00

TWA, Carolans Irish Cream Liqueur.
$6.00

TWA Collector's Series. $8.00

TWA, Lettering. $6.00

Two of a Kind California, 2007.
$1.00

Uncle Sam Brand, 1940s. $9.00

Union 76 Gas Logo. $4.50

Union Label. $1.00

Union Plaza Hotel & Casino. $1.50

Union Plaza Hotel & Casino. $2.00

United Airlines. $4.00

United Airlines Bicentennial Deck, 1976. $4.00

United Airlines, Blue Deck. $3.00

United Airlines, Gray Deck. $3.00

United States Coast Guard. $6.00

United States Flag. $4.00

United States Line, Leviathan. $7.50

United States Maps. $4.00

Universal Brand. $1.50

Universal Studios. $3.00

University of Michigan Football, 2008. $4.00

University of Pittsburgh, 1905. $75.00

Upper Michigan Copper Country, Mini Deck. $2.00

US Army, Go Army. $8.00

US Army Special Services (1). $10.00

US Army Special Services (2). $10.00

Vail Ski Resort, Colorado. $3.00

Vantage Cigarettes (1). $4.50

Vantage Cigarettes (2). $4.50

Vegas Brand Blue. $2.00

Vegas Brand Red. $2.00

Vegas Nite Roulette. $2.00

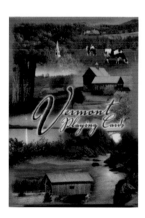

Vermont, Scenic Tourist. $3.00

Viceroy Cigarettes (1). $4.50

Viceroy Cigarettes (2). $4.50

Victory Patriot Cards, 1945. $100.00

Victory, WWII. $100.00

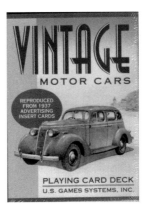

Vintage Motor Cars. $5.00

Virginia Slims, Lettering. $4.50

Wall Street Journal. $4.50

Walt Disney World. $3.00

Washington Monument.
$3.00

Welch's Grape Juice 2 Deck Set. $10.00

Werewolf, Creepy Classics. $5.00

West Virginia, Tourist. $3.00

Western Knives. $4.50

Westinghouse Washer & Dryer. $4.50

Wheat Chex Cereal. $10.00

Whist 53. $4.00

White House. $3.00

Wickes Lumber, Double Deck. $2.00

Wienermobile, Henry Ford Museum, Michigan. $4.00

Wild Animal Park. $3.00

Win Lose Draw Pinups, 1944. $35.00

Winchester Mystery House. $2.00

Winchester Western, Mallard Duck. $6.00

Winnie the Pooh, Disney. $6.00

Winston Cigarettes (1). $4.50

Winston Cigarettes (2). $4.50

Winston Cigarettes Weekends. $6.00

Winston Cigarettes, Double Deck Set. $9.00

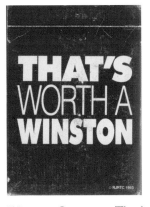

Winston Cigarettes, That's Worth A Winston. $6.00

Wisconsin, Spring Green, The House On The Rock. $2.00

Wonder Works, Tennessee. $1.00

World Poker Tour, Single Deck. $2.00

World Series Poker, Tin Set. $10.00

Yellow Pages. $3.00 Each

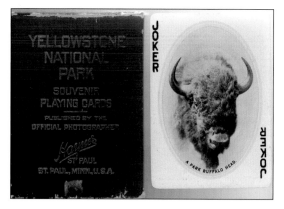

Yellow Freight. $1.00

Yellowstone National Park, Early 20th Century. $50.00

Yellowstone Park, 1925. $35.00

Zenith. $4.50

Zesta Crackers. $10.00

Main Price Guide

MAIN PRICE GUIDE

DESCRIPTION	MIB	CONDITION NEW	GOOD	STYLE
$100 Bill Replica, Canada	$2.00	$1.50	$1.00	S
$100 Bill Replica. U.S.	$2.00	$1.50	$1.00	S
101 Dalmations	$5.00	$4.00	$2.50	S
AAA Brand Playing Cards	$1.50	$1.00	$0.50	S
AAA China Gold Brand	$1.50	$1.00	$0.50	S
AAA, Various Tourist/ Driving Scenes	$4.00	$3.00	$2.00	S
A Class Brand, Made in Hong Kong	$1.50	$1.00	$0.75	S
Absolut Vodka of Sweden	$8.00	$6.00	$4.00	S
Aces Over Kings Brand, WCP Tournament, Blue or Red, NM 1949	$2.00	$1.50	$1.00	S
Acme Fast Freight Service, 2-Deck Set	$4.00	$3.00	$2.00	DD
Adobe Acrobat, Win Big, Round Deck	$6.00	$4.50	$3.00	R
Adventureland, Des Moines, Iowa, Tourist	$3.00	$2.00	$1.50	S
AE, Automotive Engineers, 2-Deck Set	$8.00	$6.00	$4.00	DD
Age of Mythology PC (Computer) Game by Microsoft	$8.00	$6.00	$4.00	S
Air Force Academy, Colorado	$5.00	$4.00	$2.50	S
Air France	$8.00	$6.00	$4.00	S
Air Jamaica, Birds in Circles	$8.00	$6.00	$4.00	S
Aircraft Recognition, 1979, U.S. Army Official Release	$12.00	$9.00	$6.00	S
Airplane Spotter, USPC, Airplane Silhouettes & Names, 1943			$50.00	S
Alabama Crimson Tide, University	$5.00	$4.00	$2.50	S
Aladdin Hotel & Casino	$2.00	$1.50	$1.00	S
Alaska Airlines, Large Jet	$8.00	$6.00	$4.00	S
Alaska, Big Dipper, Tourist	$4.00	$3.00	$2.00	S
Alaska, Brown Bear Backs, Single Deck in Bear Decorated Tin	$6.00	$4.50	$3.00	S
Alaska Bush Plane Tourist	$1.50	$1.00	$0.50	S
Alaska Railroad	$12.00	$9.00	$6.00	S
Alaska-Seattle Cruise Line	$5.00	$4.00	$2.50	S
Alcatraz Prison, San Francisco, California	$4.00	$3.00	$2.00	S
Alien Head, Green, Hoyle	$4.00	$3.00	$2.00	S
Allied Van Lines, Moving Truck	$5.00	$4.00	$2.50	S
Alverna College	$4.00	$3.00	$2.00	S
AMC Pacer, Automobile, 1970s	$8.00	$6.00	$4.00	S
American Airlines, AA in White Squares, Red & Black Squares	$5.00	$4.00	$2.50	S
American Airlines Dh-4, Biplane w. U.S. Mail	$12.50	$10.00	$7.50	S
American Airlines DH-4, Single Wing Plane, 1972	$10.00	$7.50	$5.00	S
American Airlines, Eagle and AA	$5.00	$4.00	$2.50	S
American Airlines, Eagle in Circle AA	$5.00	$4.00	$2.50	S
American Airlines, Lettering, Repeated Rows	$5.00	$4.00	$2.50	S
American Airlines, Rows of A's—Alternating Upside Down	$5.00	$4.00	$2.50	S
American Airlines, Route of the Astro Jets, Eagle and AA	$10.00	$7.50	$5.00	S
American Eagle Brand, Just Living the Dream	$5.00	$4.00	$2.50	S
American History, Piatnik, Famous Ams. On Face Cards, DD Set	$20.00	$15.00	$10.00	DD
American Indian, Corn Dancer Clown, 1900			$125.00	S
American Iron & Machine Works	$4.00	$3.00	$2.00	S
American President Lines, Eagle & Stars	$8.00	$6.00	$4.00	S
American States Insurance	$2.00	$1.50	$1.00	S
American Yacht Club, Sailing Flag	$4.00	$3.00	$2.00	S
Amma Co., Military Caricature Face Cards, 1941			$75.00	S
Amstel Beer	$8.00	$6.00	$4.00	S
Amtrak, Railroad	$6.00	$4.50	$3.00	S
Anaheim Angels	$6.00	$4.50	$3.00	S
Anaheim Mighty Ducks	$6.00	$4.50	$3.00	S
Angel Fire Resort, Tourist	$2.00	$1.50	$1.00	S
Anheiser-Busch, Logo, Double Deck Set	$10.00	$7.50	$5.00	DD
Animal Kingdom, Walt Disney World, Florida Tourist, Plastic Case	$4.00	$3.00	$2.00	S
Ante by Umbra, Unusual Oblong—Long Narrow Deck, Plastic Case	$8.00	$6.00	$4.00	U
Antique Motor Cars, 1920s Reproduction	$5.00	$4.00	$2.50	S
Apollo Brand, National Card Co., 1890			$75.00	S
Apple Barn Tourist	$1.50	$1.00	$0.50	S
Aquarius the Water Bearer, Zodiac Sign, 1960s	$10.00	$7.50	$5.00	S
Aries the Ram, Zodiac Sign, 1960s	$10.00	$7.50	$5.00	S
Aristocrat Brand	$1.50	$1.00	$0.50	S
Arizona, Cactus Design, Tourist	$4.00	$3.00	$2.00	S
Arizona Cardinals	$6.00	$4.50	$3.00	S
Arizona Diamondbacks	$6.00	$4.50	$3.00	S
Arizona Razorbacks, Go Hogs, University	$5.00	$4.00	$2.50	S
Arizona Tourist, Parks	$1.50	$1.00	$0.50	S
Arizona Tourist, Roadrunner	$1.50	$1.00	$0.50	S
Arizona Tourist, Sedona	$1.50	$1.00	$0.50	S
Arizona Wildcats, University	$5.00	$4.00	$2.50	S

Arkansas Razorbacks, University	$5.00	$4.00	$2.50	S
Arrow Schnapps	$8.00	$6.00	$4.00	S
Art Deck, Art Detail by Piatnik	$8.00	$6.00	$4.00	S
Art Deck, Bridgeman Art Library, Monet Bridge Backs, Piatnik	$8.00	$6.00	$4.00	S
Art Deck, Impression Masterpieces by Piatnik	$8.00	$6.00	$4.00	S
Art Deck, The Nude, Piatnik	$8.00	$6.00	$4.00	S
Art Deck, Oriental, Dream of Red Mansions, Art Box	$8.00	$6.00	$4.00	S
Art Deck, Portrait Pack, Piatnik	$8.00	$6.00	$4.00	S
Art Deck, 13 Modern Masters, Art on Cards	$8.00	$6.00	$4.00	S
Astronomical Cards by Piatnik	$6.00	$4.50	$3.00	S
Atlanta Braves	$6.00	$4.50	$3.00	S
Atlanta Falcons	$6.00	$4.50	$3.00	S
Atlanta Hawks	$6.00	$4.50	$3.00	S
Atlanta Olympics, 1996	$5.00	$4.00	$2.50	S
Atlanta Olympics, 1996, 2-Deck Set, Vinyl Case	$15.00	$11.00	$7.50	
Atlanta Thrashers	$6.00	$4.50	$3.00	S
Atlanta Underground, Railroad	$6.00	$4.50	$3.00	S
Atlantic City, Framed Tourist Scenes, Cardboard Box	$4.00	$3.00	$2.00	S
Atlantic City, Gambling Icons, 1970s	$1.50	$1.00	$0.50	S
Atlantic Coast Line, Railroad	$12.00	$9.00	$6.00	S
Atlantis, Casino	$2.00	$1.50	$1.00	S
Atomic Fire Ball, Red Hot Quality Candies	$8.00	$6.00	$4.00	S
Auburn Esso Service, Pin-Up Girl on Couch, 1960		$30.00	$20.00	S
Auburn Tigers, University	$5.00	$4.00	$2.50	S
Authors	$5.00	$4.00	$2.50	S
Authors, Black	$5.00	$4.00	$2.50	S
Authors, Classic	$5.00	$4.00	$2.50	S
Authors, Mystery	$5.00	$4.00	$2.50	S
Authors, Science Fiction	$5.00	$4.00	$2.50	S
Authors, 20th Century	$5.00	$4.00	$2.50	S
Authors, Women	$5.00	$4.00	$2.50	S
AutoWorld, Theme Park	$3.00	$2.00	$1.50	S
Avi, Casino	$2.00	$1.50	$1.00	S
Aviator, Brand	$2.00	$1.50	$1.00	S
Aviator, Brand, Blue Stamp Seal, 1940s	$3.00	$2.00	$1.50	S
Avis, Name Repeated 16 times in Rectangles, We Rent GM Cars	$5.00	$4.00	$2.50	S
Aztec Casino	$2.00	$1.50	$1.00	S
B & O, Railroad	$12.00	$9.00	$6.00	S
Bacardi Rum	$8.00	$6.00	$4.00	S
Bacardi Summer of Rum	$5.00	$4.00	$2.50	S
Bailey's Irish Cream	$10.00	$7.50	$5.00	S
Bally's, Casino	$2.00	$1.50	$1.00	S
Baltimore Colts	$8.00	$6.00	$4.00	S
Baltimore Orioles	$6.00	$4.50	$3.00	S
Baltimore Ravens	$6.00	$4.50	$3.00	S
Bambi, Disney Film Version	$12.00	$9.00	$6.00	S
Bangor & Aroostook Railroad, Northern Maine	$8.00	$6.00	$4.00	S
Banque Nat'l Mundi, Belgium Bank, 1970	$8.00	$6.00	$4.00	S
Barclay's London Dry Gin	$8.00	$6.00	$4.00	S
Barton Brand	$1.50	$1.00	$0.75	S
Baseball, Round Mini Deck	$1.50	$1.00	$0.75	R,M
Basic Cigarettes, Various Pack Designs	$6.00	$4.50	$3.00	S
Basketball, Round Mini Deck	$1.50	$1.00	$0.75	R,M
Batman, Animated, Cartoon	$8.00	$6.00	$4.00	S
Batman, Animated, Cartoon, Mini Deck	$4.00	$3.00	$2.00	M
Batman, Bat Logo	$12.00	$9.00	$6.00	S
Batman Begins	$5.00	$4.00	$2.50	S
Batman, Movie, Jack Nicholson Joker, Michael Keaton Batman	$20.00	$17.50	$15.00	S
Batman Returns	$5.00	$4.00	$2.50	S
Beachcraft, Gold Trim, Double Deck Set	$8.00	$6.00	$4.00	DD
The Beatles, Yellow Submarine, Australian	$16.00	$12.00	$8.00	S
Bee Brand Club Special	$2.00	$1.50	$1.00	S
Bee Brand Club Special, Casino Quality, Jumbo Index	$2.00	$1.50	$1.00	S
Bee Brand, #92, 1950s	$4.00	$3.00	$2.00	S
Bee Brand Squeezers, #92, NYCC Co., 1 Joker, 1890			$100.00	S
Beggar's Opera House, England, 1978 (reproduction of 1730 Deck)	$20.00	$15.00	$10.00	S
Bell Telephone	$10.00	$7.50	$5.00	S
Bellagio, Casino	$2.00	$1.50	$1.00	S
Belle of Louisville, Large Paddle-Wheeler	$8.00	$6.00	$4.00	S
Bell's Finest Old Scotch Whisky	$10.00	$7.50	$5.00	S
Ben & Jerry's Ice Cream	$5.00	$4.00	$2.50	S
Ben Hur Life, Building, Insurance	$4.00	$3.00	$2.00	S
Benson & Hedges, Cigarettes, Various Pack Designs	$6.00	$4.50	$3.00	S
Bertola Cream Sherry	$10.00	$7.50	$5.00	S
Betty Boop	$10.00	$7.50	$5.00	S
Betty Boop, Single Deck in Tin	$12.00	$9.00	$6.00	S
Beverly Hills Country Club, Martini Glass w. Olive, Double Deck Set	$6.00	$4.50	$3.00	DD
B.F. Goodrich, Industrial Products	$4.00	$3.00	$2.00	S
Bicycle, 125th Anniversary, 2010	$2.00	$1.50	$1.00	S
Bicycle, Bicycles (2-Wheelers) Repeated, Double Deck Set	$8.00	$6.00	$4.00	DD
Bicycle Brand, Acorn Backs	$10.00	$7.50	$5.00	S
Bicycle Brand, Black & Gray Special Edition	$3.00	$2.00	$1.50	S
Bicycle Brand, Black & White Special Edition	$3.00	$2.00	$1.50	S
Bicycle Brand, Clear Design	$3.00	$2.00	$1.50	S
Bicycle Brand, Mini Deck, Plastic Case	$3.00	$2.00	$1.50	M
Bicycle, Jumbo Index	$2.00	$1.50	$1.00	S
Bicycle #86, 1920s–1930s	$12.50	$10.00	$7.50	S
Bicycle #86, 1940s–1950s	$10.00	$7.50	$5.00	DD
Bicycle, #808, USPCC, 1895 (1890s–early 1900s issue)			$85.00	S
Bicycle, #808, USPCC, 1910 (1910s–1930s)			$75.00	S
Bicycle #808, USPCC, 1940s–1950s Issue War Bonds	$40.00	$30.00	$20.00	S
Bicycle #8082, Jumbo Size, 7.5" x 4.5" Deck	$12.00	$9.00	$6.00	J
Bicycle, 48-Card Pinochle Deck	$1.50	$1.00	$0.75	P
Bicycle, Red Canasta Box, Double Deck Set, 1960s	$10.00	$7.50	$5.00	DD
Bicycle Rider Back, 4 Bicycle 2010 Special Edition	$3.00	$2.00	$1.50	S
Bicycle Rider Back, Red or Blue, Modern	$1.50	$1.00	$0.50	S
Bicycle Rider Back, Russell & Morgan Co., 1890 Deck			$475.00	S
Bicycle Rider Backs, 2-Deck Set in Tin	$12.00	$9.00	$6.00	DD
Bicycle Tall Stacks, Steam Paddlewheeler, 1950s & Older	$12.00	$9.00	$6.00	S
Bicycle Tall Stacks, Steam Paddlewheeler, 1960s–Up	$5.00	$4.00	$2.50	S

Big Ben Clock Tower, London, Tourist	$4.00	$3.00	$2.00	S
Big Ben Roll Cut Smoking Tobacco, 1 Joker, 1920s			$50.00	S
Big Boy, Restaurant	$8.00	$6.00	$4.00	S
Big Sky Country, Montana	$4.00	$3.00	$2.00	S
Bijou #1 Brand, USPC, Plaid w. Coat of Arms, 1930	$75.00	$60.00	$50.00	S
Binion's, Casino	$2.00	$1.50	$1.00	S
Biscuits Lefevre-Utile Mucha, Piatnik Double Deck Set	$12.00	$9.00	$6.00	DD
Bit O'Honey Candy	$12.00	$9.00	$6.00	S
BJ Engineered Tools	$3.00	$2.00	$1.50	S
Black & White Old Scotch Whiskey	$10.00	$7.50	$5.00	S
Black & White Old Scotch Whiskey, Scottie Dogs, 1930s		$75.00	$50.00	S
Black Label Beer	$10.00	$7.50	$5.00	S
Black Velvet Whiskey, Various Models in Black Dress	$10.00	$7.50	$5.00	S
Blatz Beer, Can Shaped	$10.00	$7.50	$5.00	S
Blue Bonnet, Margarine, Lad's Head in Bonnet, Repeated on Opp. Side	$10.00	$7.50	$5.00	S
Blue Cross, Blue Shield, 7 Steps to Good Health	$4.00	$3.00	$2.00	S
Blue Ribbon Band, Russell Playing Cards, Gold Edge	$10.00	$7.50	$5.00	S
Boardwalk, Casino	$2.00	$1.50	$1.00	S
Bob Evans Farms or Restaurants	$8.00	$6.00	$4.00	S
Boblo Island, Amusement Park	$4.00	$3.00	$2.00	S
Boeing 707–1959, Jet	$12.50	$10.00	$7.50	S
Boeing 727–1964, Jet	$12.50	$10.00	$7.50	S
Boeing 747–1970, Jet	$12.50	$10.00	$7.50	S
Boeing Stratoliner—1940, Jet	$16.00	$12.00	$8.00	S
Boheme, Cruise Lines, Large Ship	$6.00	$4.50	$3.00	S
Bohemia, Piatnik, Double Deck Set	$12.00	$9.00	$6.00	DD
Bohemia Moravia, Piatnik, Double Deck Set	$12.00	$9.00	$6.00	DD
Boomtown, Casino	$2.00	$1.50	$1.00	S
Border Collies & Sheep	$1.00	$0.75	$0.50	S
Boston & Maine, Railroad	$8.00	$6.00	$4.00	S
Boston Bruins	$6.00	$4.50	$3.00	S
Boston Celtics	$6.00	$4.50	$3.00	S
Boston Red Sox	$6.00	$4.50	$3.00	S
Boston Souvenir Deck, Chisholm Bros., 1899			$75.00	S
Botticelli, Piatnik, Double Deck Set	$12.00	$9.00	$6.00	DD
Bow Wow Bone-Shaped Cards by Umbra, Plastic Case	$8.00	$6.00	$4.00	U
Boy's Town Scene, 1955	$50.00	$35.00	$25.00	S
BP Gas, Mini Deck	$5.00	$4.00	$2.50	M
Braniff International, White Lettering	$4.00	$3.00	$2.00	S
Branson, Missouri, Tourist, Plastic Case, Various Designs	$4.00	$3.00	$2.00	S
Bridge Brand, Woolworth Woolco, Made in Hong Kong	$1.50	$1.00	$0.75	S
Bristol Cigarettes	$6.00	$4.50	$3.00	S
Britania, Large Cruise Ship	$6.00	$4.50	$3.00	S
British Airways	$8.00	$6.00	$4.00	S
Bronner's Christmas Wonderland, Souvenir Deck in Plastic Case	$4.00	$3.00	$2.00	S
Bubba Gump Gumpisms	$5.00	$4.00	$2.50	S
Buckinghan Palace, Changing of the Guard	$2.00	$1.50	$1.00	S
Buck's Brand, Buck on Backs & on Jokers too	$1.50	$1.00	$0.50	S
Bud Light, Beer Logo, Various Styles	$6.00	$4.50	$3.00	S
Bud Light, Spuds Mackenzie Dog	$10.00	$7.50	$5.00	S
Budweiser, Beer Logo, Various Styles	$6.00	$4.50	$3.00	S
Budweiser Beer, 2 Deck Set in Tin	$15.00	$11.50	$7.50	DD
Budweiser, Clydesdales	$8.00	$6.00	$4.00	S
Budweiser, King of Beers, Lettering Only	$6.00	$4.50	$3.00	S
Budweiser, Lizards	$8.00	$6.00	$4.00	S
Budweiser, Logo, House, etc., Various Designs	$8.00	$6.00	$4.00	S
Budweiser, The Budweiser Girl (Various Women in Gowns)	$15.00	$12.50	$7.50	S
Budweiser, Top View of 24-Pack Case	$8.00	$6.00	$4.00	S
Buffalo & Niagara Falls, New York, Barnam & Sons Souvenir, c. 1910		$100.00		S
Buffalo, Wyoming, Herd of Buffalo, Tourist	$4.00	$3.00	$2.00	S
Buffalo Bill, Pawnee Bill, 1 Joker, 1880s			$1,000	S
Buffalo Bills	$6.00	$4.50	$3.00	S
Buffalo Sabres	$6.00	$4.50	$3.00	S
Buffy the Vampire Slayer, TV Series	$12.00	$9.00	$6.00	S
Bugs Bunny, Looney Tunes, 1990s	$8.00	$6.00	$4.00	S
Buick 50th Anniversary, 1903–1953	$8.00	$6.00	$4.00	S
Bull Dog Squeezers	$2.00	$1.50	$1.00	S
Bullfighter, Clemente Jacques	$50.00	$40.00	$30.00	S
Bumble Bee Tuna	$8.00	$6.00	$4.00	S
Burlington Northern, Railroad	$8.00	$6.00	$4.00	S
Burlington Route, Railroad	$8.00	$6.00	$4.00	S
Burlington, Vista Dome Zephyr, 1940s	$75.00	$50.00	$35.00	S
Busch Beer	$8.00	$6.00	$4.00	S
Bush, George W., W Bathing Suit Deck	$5.00	$4.00	$2.50	S
Bushmills Irish Whiskey	$10.00	$7.50	$5.00	S
Buster Brown, Cartoon Characters, USPC, 1 Joker, 1906			$75.00	S
Butler Brand Paper, Globe, Worldwide Distribution	$4.00	$3.00	$2.00	S
C & O For Progress, Railroad	$6.00	$4.00	$3.00	S
C & O Railroad, East West Via Washington, USPC, 1900			$75.00	S
C & O Railroad Scene, 1900			$75.00	S
Cabelas	$3.00	$2.00	$1.50	S
Cabinet Brand, Russell & Morgan Ptg. Co., 1890			$150.00	S
Caesars Palace, Casino	$2.00	$1.50	$1.00	S
Calgary Flames	$6.00	$4.50	$3.00	S
California Angels	$6.00	$4.50	$3.00	S
California Baccarat, Casino	$2.00	$1.50	$1.00	S
California Hotel & Casino	$2.00	$1.50	$1.00	S
California Poppy Flower Souvenir Deck, Reider, 1911			$75.00	S
California Souvenir Deck, M Reider, 1 Joker, 1908			$150.00	S
California Tourist, Early 20th Century			$50.00	S
California Western Railroad, The Skunk Line	$6.00	$4.50	$3.00	S
California Wine Depot, 1 Joker, 1890s			$100.00	S
California Zephyr, Railroad, Mountain Scene	$20.00	$15.00	$10.00	S
Calvert, Whiskey	$6.00	$4.50	$3.00	S

Calvert, Various Brands, Whiskey or Gin	$6.00	$4.50	$3.00	S
Camel Cigarettes, 23 Small Camels, Dark one in Center	$6.00	$4.50	$3.00	S
Camel Cigarettes, Joe Camel, Various Designs	$6.00	$4.50	$3.00	S
Camel Cigarettes, Pack Design, Various Styles	$8.00	$6.00	$4.00	S
Camel Cigarettes, Turkish & Domestic Blends, Pack Design	$8.00	$6.00	$4.00	S
Camp Snoopy, Various Locations, Tourist	$6.00	$4.50	$3.00	S
Campbell's Alphabet Soup, Meatball & Chicken Double Set	$15.00	$12.00	$7.50	DD
Campbell's Chunky Soup	$6.00	$4.50	$3.00	S
Canada, Maple Leaf Flag, Tourist, Plastic Case	$4.00	$3.00	$2.00	S
Canada, Maple Leaf Flag, Tourist, Mini Deck, Plastic Case	$3.00	$2.00	$1.50	M
Canadian Club, Lettering Only	$6.00	$4.50	$3.00	S
Canadian Club Imported Whiskey, Bottle	$8.00	$6.00	$4.00	S
Canadian National Railways	$8.00	$6.00	$4.00	S
Canadian National Railways, 1940s	$60.00	$45.00	$30.00	S
Canadian Pacific, Railroad	$8.00	$6.00	$4.00	S
Cancer the Crab, Zodiac Sign, 1960s	$10.00	$7.50	$5.00	S
Canon E70 Canovision Camera	$4.00	$3.00	$2.00	S
Cape Cod Bay, Massachusetts	$4.00	$3.00	$2.00	S
Cape Coral Gardens, Florida	$4.00	$3.00	$2.00	S
Capital Airlines Viscount	$4.00	$3.00	$2.00	S
Capricorn the Goat, Zodiac Sign, 1960s	$10.00	$7.50	$5.00	S
Captain Morgan Rum	$8.00	$6.00	$4.00	S
Care Bears, Cartoon	$6.00	$4.50	$3.00	S
Caribbean Cruise Lines, Flag	$6.00	$4.50	$3.00	S
Carling Black Label Beer, Can-Shape	$10.00	$7.50	$5.00	S
Carling Stag Beer, Can-Shape	$10.00	$7.50	$5.00	S
Carnival Cruise, New Orleans, 1926			$50.00	S
Carnival, Large Cruise Ship	$5.00	$4.00	$2.50	S
Carnival, The Fun Ship, Lettering Only	$4.00	$3.00	$2.00	S
Carnivale Festivale Mardi Gras. Cruiseline, Lettering Only	$5.00	$4.00	$2.50	S
Carnivale Festivale Mardi Gras, Cruisline, Ship	$6.00	$4.50	$3.00	S
Carolans Irish Cream Liquer, Bottle & Cordial	$8.00	$6.00	$4.00	S
Carolina Hurricanes	$6.00	$4.50	$3.00	S
Carolina Panthers	$6.00	$4.50	$3.00	S
Casablanca, Rick's Café Americain, Austria, Movie, 2004 Reissue	$12.00	$9.00	$6.00	DD
Casa Loma, Toronto, Canada, Tourist, Plastic Case	$4.00	$3.00	$2.00	S
Casanova, Becat, French Fancy Nudes	$300.00	$225.00	$150.00	S
Casino Card Club San Jose	$2.00	$1.50	$1.00	S
Casino Royale James Bond Film Double Set	$10.00	$7.50	$5.00	DD
Castaways, Casino	$2.00	$1.50	$1.00	S
Castle Rock, Michigan, Tourist, Cardboard Box	$4.00	$3.00	$2.00	S
Cat & Ball Brand, Taiwan	$2.00	$1.50	$1.00	S
Caterpillar Earthmoving Equipment	$8.00	$6.00	$4.00	S
Caterpillar Equipment, Large Equipment	$8.00	$6.00	$4.00	S
Cavalier Cigarettes	$6.00	$4.50	$3.00	S
Cedar Point, Amusement Park, Various Designs	$4.00	$3.00	$2.00	S
Centennial Olympic Games, 1896–1996 Anniversary	$6.00	$4.50	$3.00	S
Central Railroad Company of New Jersey	$4.00	$3.00	$2.00	S
Century of Progress, Chicago, 1933		$30.00	$20.00	S
Champion Brand, Casino Style, Belgium—Carta Mundi	$2.00	$1.50	$1.00	S
Champion, Repeated in Globes (Champion Spark Plug)	$5.00	$4.00	$2.50	S
Champion Spark Plugs, Spark Plug on Backs	$8.00	$6.00	$4.00	S
Charlotte Hornets	$6.00	$4.50	$3.00	S
Cheer-Up, Hospital Cartoons, 1960	$10.00	$7.50	$5.00	S
Cheetos with Chester Cheetah	$6.00	$4.50	$3.00	S
Cherchez lafemme, French, Nude, 1940s	$30.00	$25.00	$20.00	S
Chess, Board Game, 1 Joker, 1935			$100.00	S
Chessie System, Railroad	$8.00	$6.00	$4.00	S
Chester Cheetah, Cheetos Mascot	$6.00	$4.50	$3.00	S
Chevrolet, 1962	$6.00	$4.50	$3.00	S
Chevrolet Erotosi, 1966 Fleet Pack, 48-Card Pinochle Deck	$6.00	$4.50	$3.00	P
Chevrolet Motor Company, 2-Deck Set in Tin	$10.00	$7.50	$5.00	DD
Chevron Oil Company, Company Logo	$8.00	$6.00	$4.00	S
Chevron Oil Company, Save the Dinosaurs, Conserve Energy	$10.00	$7.50	$5.00	S
Chex Cereal, Corn or Rice Chex	$10.00	$7.50	$5.00	S
Chicago & Eastern Illinois Route, Railroad	$8.00	$6.00	$4.00	S
Chicago Bears	$6.00	$4.50	$3.00	S
Chicago Blackhawks	$6.00	$4.50	$2.00	S
Chicago Bulls	$6.00	$4.50	$3.00	S
Chicago Bulls, Michael Jordan	$16.00	$12.00	$8.00	S
Chicago Bulls, Michael Jordan, Double Deck Special Edition	$35.00	$25.00	$17.50	DD
Chicago Burlington Route, Railroad	$8.00	$6.00	$4.00	S
Chicago Cubs	$6.00	$4.50	$3.00	S
Chicago, Milwaukee & St. Paul Railroad, 1910			$75.00	S
Chicago Missouri and Western Railway	$8.00	$6.00	$4.00	S
Chicago, Tiny City Icons, Tourist, Plastic Case	$4.00	$3.00	$2.00	S
Chicago, Various Tourist	$4.00	$3.00	$2.00	S
Chicago White Sox	$6.00	$4.50	$3.00	S
Chicago World's Fair, Walgreen Building, Double Deck Set, 1933	$60.00	$45.00	$30.00	DD
Chicago World's Fair, 1934 A Century of Progress	$30.00	$22.50	$15.00	S
China, Brand, Basic "Made in China" Generic	$1.00	$0.75	$0.50	S
China, Shanghai Hotel	$1.00	$0.75	$0.50	S
China Shanghai Museum	$4.00	$3.00	$2.00	S
Chinese Folk Customs in Tin	$4.00	$3.00	$2.00	S
Chinese Historical Spots in Tin	$4.00	$3.00	$2.00	S
Chinese Mao Tourist Deck in Tin	$4.00	$3.00	$2.00	S
Chinese Terra Cotta Soldiers	$4.00	$3.00	$2.00	S
Chinese Tiny Deck, One Inch by One and a Half Inch	$0.50	$0.35	$0.25	T
Chinese Xian Souvenir	$4.00	$3.00	$2.00	S
Chippendales, Male Dancers, 1987	$8.00	$6.00	$4.00	S

Chlor-Trimeton Tablets, Allergy & Decongestant, Lettering Only	$4.00	$3.00	$2.00	S
Christmas Cards; Elf, Tree, Reindeer, & Snowman Suits	$8.00	$6.00	$4.00	U
A Christmas Carol, Dickens, Double Set	$6.00	$4.50	$3.00	DD
Christmas Holiday, Green or Red	$2.00	$1.50	$1.00	S
A Christmas Story, Turner/ WB Film, Double Deck Set in Tin	$12.00	$9.00	$6.00	DD
Christmas Snowman Shaped Cards, 2006	$3.00	$2.00	$1.50	S
Christmas Tree Shaped Cards, 2006	$3.00	$2.00	$1.50	S
Chunky Soup, Campbells Read to Serve, Can Design	$8.00	$6.00	$4.00	S
Cigar Poker by Piatnik	$6.00	$4.50	$3.00	S
Cincinnati Bengals	$6.00	$4.50	$3.00	S
Cincinnati Reds	$6.00	$4.50	$3.00	S
Cincinnati Reds, Tiny Deck, 1 7/8" x 1 1/4"	$4.00	$3.00	$2.00	T
Cincinnati Zoo, White Tiger, Tourist, Plastic Case	$4.00	$3.00	$2.00	S
Cinderella Mini Deck	$3.00	$2.00	$1.50	M
Circus Circus, Casino	$2.00	$1.50	$1.00	S
The Citadel, The Military College of the South	$6.00	$4.50	$3.00	S
CITGO, Orange Triangle Logo	$8.00	$6.00	$4.00	S
CITGO, Cities Service Co.	$2.00	$1.50	$1.00	S
Citi-Bank	$3.00	$2.00	$1.50	S
Civil War, Confederate Generals, 1980s	$5.00	$4.00	$2.50	S
Civil War, Face Themes, American Land Co., 1860s			$1,000	S
Civil War, Generals (both sides), 1980s	$5.00	$4.00	$2.50	S
Civil War, Union Generals, 1980s	$5.00	$4.00	$2.50	S
The Claridge, Casino	$2.00	$1.50	$1.00	S
Clemson Tigers, University	$5.00	$4.00	$2.50	S
Cleveland Browns	$6.00	$4.50	$3.00	S
Cleveland Cavaliers	$6.00	$4.50	$3.00	S
Cleveland Indians	$6.00	$4.50	$3.00	S
Clifden, County Galway, Ireland, Harp Ace of Spades	$5.00	$4.00	$2.50	S
Clinchfield Railroad	$4.00	$3.00	$2.00	S
Club Cal, Casino	$2.00	$1.50	$1.00	S
CN Rail, Railroad, Engine	$20.00	$15.00	$10.00	S
Coca-Cola, Advertising Girl, Brown & Bigelow, 1943			$100.00	S
Coca-Cola, Many Designs, Modern	$6.00	$4.50	$3.00	S
Coca-Cola, Various Models in Dress and/or Hats, 1950s–1960s	$15.00	$10.00	$7.50	S
Coca-Cola, Various Models in Dress and/or Hats, 1970s - Up	$7.50	$5.50	$3.75	S
Coca-Cola, 2 Deck Set in Tin, Many Modern Designs	$12.00	$9.00	$6.00	DD
Coca-Cola, 2 Deck Set W/O Tin, Many Modern Designs	$10.00	$7.50	$5.00	DD
Coca-Cola, WWII Fly Girl, 1940s	$100.00	$75.00	$50.00	S
Colorado Avalanche	$6.00	$4.50	$3.00	S
Colorado Rockies	$6.00	$4.50	$3.00	S
Colt Firearms, Snake Eyes, 1989	$6.00	$4.50	$3.00	S
Columbia River, Oregon, 1909			$200.00	S
Columbian Exposition, Winters, Hand-Drawn Pictures, 1893			$150.00	S
Columbus Blue Jackets	$6.00	$4.50	$3.00	S
Combat Vehicle Identification, 1985	$10.00	$7.50	$5.00	S
Compagnie Maritime Belge, Cruise Lines	$5.00	$4.00	$2.50	S
The Concord, Concord Jet	$12.00	$9.00	$6.00	S
Confederate Flag	$4.00	$3.00	$2.00	S
Congress Brand, Russell & Morgan, 1870s			$75.00	S
Congress Brand, USPC, Indian Maiden Minnehaha, 1947		$30.00	$20.00	S
Congress Brand, Cel-U-Tone Packaging, 1950s–1960s	$4.00	$3.00	$2.00	S
Congress 606 Brand, Barn Scene, 1920s			$20.00	S
Congress 606 Brand, 48-Card Pinochle in Leather Case, 1930s	$12.00	$9.00	$6.00	S
Congress 606 Brand, Russell & Morgan, Girl w. Spyglass, 1920s			$75.00	S
Congress 606 Brand, Russell & Morgan, Girl (Rose) in Cameo, 1905			$85.00	S
Connecticut, Sailing Ship, Tourist	$5.00	$4.00	$2.50	S
Conoco, Hottest Brand Going	$6.00	$4.50	$3.00	S
Consolidated Pinochle 48-Card Deck, 1885			$25.00	S
Conrail, Railroad	$8.00	$6.00	$4.00	S
Contac Decongestant Tablets	$10.00	$7.50	$5.00	S
Continental Airlines, Circle Logo, Various Designs	$5.00	$4.00	$2.50	S
Continental, Alternating Rows of Circles & Continental's	$5.00	$4.00	$2.50	S
Converse Carlisle Coal Co.	$5.00	$4.00	$2.50	S
Cool Whip, Tub Cover in Small Circle, Scrolling	$8.00	$6.00	$4.00	S
Coors, Lettering Only	$6.00	$4.50	$3.00	S
Coors Beer, Logo	$8.00	$6.00	$4.00	S
Coors Light Beer, Logo	$8.00	$6.00	$4.00	S
Coricidin D Decongestant Cold Relief Tablets	$6.00	$4.50	$3.00	S
Corn Palace, South Dakota	$5.00	$4.00	$2.50	S
Cotton Belt Route, Railroad	$8.00	$6.00	$4.00	S
Country Music, Best of, 54 Artists on Cards	$8.00	$6.00	$4.00	S
Country Music, Heather Products, 1967	$20.00	$15.00	$10.00	S
Country Music Hall of Fame, Nashville, TN	$3.00	$2.00	$1.50	S
Courvoisier Brandy	$6.00	$4.50	$3.00	S
Cowboys	$3.00	$2.00	$1.50	S
Cracker Barrel, Restaurant	$8.00	$6.00	$4.00	S
Cracker Jack, Snack Box Design	$8.00	$6.00	$4.00	S
Crayola Crayons, Cards can be Colored (B & W Pictures)	$8.00	$6.00	$4.00	S
Crazy Horse Monument in Tin	$4.00	$3.00	$2.00	S
Cream of Wheat	$8.00	$6.00	$4.00	S
Credit Union, Where You Belong	$2.00	$1.50	$1.00	S
Crested Ten Irish Whiskey	$10.00	$7.50	$5.00	S
Crocodile Hunter, Steve Irwin, TV Show	$6.00	$4.50	$3.00	S
Crooked Deck, Wide Deck to Accommodate Crooked Card Design	$6.00	$4.50	$3.00	U
Crown Band, Gold Foil Box, 1960s	$8.00	$6.00	$4.00	S
Crown Royal Whiskey	$8.00	$6.00	$4.00	S
CS2 3M Communication Systems, 1969	$2.00	$1.50	$1.00	S
CSX Corp., Railroad	$8.00	$6.00	$4.00	S
CU Republic Airlines	$4.00	$3.00	$2.00	S
Cunard Line, Modern, Cruiseline	$5.00	$4.00	$2.50	S

Cunard Line, Steamship, Forman & Sons, 1900		$100.00	$75.00	S
Cutty Sark Scots Whisket, Girl in Bathing Suit	$12.00	$8.00	$6.00	S
CVS Brand	$2.00	$1.50	$1.00	S
Da Vinci	$8.00	$6.00	$4.00	S
Daffy Duck, Looney Tunes, 1990s	$8.00	$6.00	$4.00	S
Daiquiri Rum	$6.00	$4.50	$3.00	S
Dairy Queen	$4.00	$3.00	$2.00	S
Dallas Cowboys	$6.00	$4.50	$3.00	S
Dallas Cowboys Cheerleaders, Large Blue Star	$4.00	$3.00	$2.00	S
Dallas Mavericks	$6.00	$4.50	$3.00	S
Dallas Stars	$6.00	$4.50	$3.00	S
Dayton Ohio, Airplane Museum	$5.00	$4.00	$2.50	S
Delaware, Small Wonder, Tourist	$4.00	$3.00	$2.00	S
Delco-Remy Engineering & Research Center, Large Building	$4.00	$3.00	$2.00	S
Delta Air Lines, Atlanta, City Scene	$10.00	$7.50	$5.00	S
Delta Air Lines, Atlanta, Lady in Dress	$10.00	$7.50	$5.00	S
Delta Air Lines, Bermuda, Tropical Beach Scene	$10.00	$7.50	$5.00	S
Delta Air Lines, Boston, City Scene	$10.00	$7.50	$5.00	S
Delta Air Lines, Chicago, City Scene	$10.00	$7.50	$5.00	S
Delta Air Lines, Chicago, Man Drinking & Smoking	$10.00	$7.50	$5.00	S
Delta Air Lines, Dallas/Fort Worth, City Skyline	$10.00	$7.50	$5.00	S
Delta Air Lines, Detroit, Man & Car	$10.00	$7.50	$5.00	S
Delta Air Lines, 50th Anniversary, 1929–1979	$10.00	$7.50	$5.00	S
Delta Air Lines, Florida West Coast, Fishing & Beach Scene	$10.00	$7.50	$5.00	S
Delta Air Lines, Globe	$5.00	$4.00	$2.50	S
Delta Air Lines, Houston, City Scene	$10.00	$7.50	$5.00	S
Delta Air Lines, Houston, Oil Worker	$10.00	$7.50	$5.00	S
Delta Air Lines, Las Vegas, The Strip	$10.00	$7.50	$5.00	S
Delta Air Lines, Lines or Lettering Only	$5.00	$4.00	$2.50	S
Delta Air Lines, Los Angeles, Actress in Evening Gown	$10.00	$7.50	$5.00	S
Delta Air Lines, Los Angeles, Cleopatra & Bobby (Policeman)	$10.00	$7.50	$5.00	S
Delta Air Lines, Miami, Sailboats & City Skyline	$10.00	$7.50	$5.00	S
Delta Air Lines, Miami & Fort Lauderdale, Beach Scene	$10.00	$7.50	$5.00	S
Delta Air Lines, New England, Old Village Scene	$10.00	$7.50	$5.00	S
Delta Air Lines, New Orleans, City Scene	$10.00	$7.50	$5.00	S
Delta Air Lines, New Orleans, French Quarter Scene	$10.00	$7.50	$5.00	S
Delta Air Lines, New Orleans, Jazz Trumpeter	$10.00	$7.50	$5.00	S
Delta Air Lines, New York, City Scene	$10.00	$7.50	$5.00	S
Delta Air Lines, New York, Policeman Blowing Whistle	$10.00	$7.50	$5.00	S
Delta Air Lines, New York,				
Statue of Liberty	$10.00	$7.50	$5.00	S
Delta Air Lines, Puerto Rico, Lady in Veil	$10.00	$7.50	$5.00	S
Delta Air Lines, San Francisco, Oriental Woman & Street Scene	$10.00	$7.50	$5.00	S
Delta Air Lines, San Francisco, Street Car Scene	$10.00	$7.50	$5.00	S
Delta Air Lines, Various Lettering, Triangle, Line, & Logo Designs	$5.00	$4.00	$2.50	S
Delta Air Lines, Washington, Jefferson Memorial	$10.00	$7.50	$5.00	S
Delta Air Lines, Washington, Various Monuments	$10.00	$7.50	$5.00	S
Delta Line, Cruise Ship	$6.00	$4.50	$3.00	S
Denver Broncos	$6.00	$4.50	$3.00	S
Denver Nuggets	$6.00	$4.50	$3.00	S
Desert Inn, Casino	$2.00	$1.50	$1.00	S
Detroit Lions	$6.00	$4.50	$3.00	S
Detroit Pistons	$6.00	$4.50	$3.00	S
Detroit Red Wings	$6.00	$4.50	$3.00	S
Detroit Tigers	$6.00	$4.50	$3.00	S
Detroit Tigers Hero Deck	$5.00	$4.00	$2.50	S
Dewars White Label Whisky	$10.00	$7.50	$5.00	S
Dial Soap	$8.00	$6.00	$4.00	S
Diamond Salt	$20.00	$15.00	$10.00	S
Diet Coke, Soft Drink	$6.00	$4.50	$3.00	S
Diet Pepsi, Soft Drink	$6.00	$4.50	$3.00	S
Dinosaurs, The Age Of, T-Rex Cover	$5.00	$4.00	$2.50	S
Discovery Channel, Blue Butterfly Backs	$6.00	$4.50	$3.00	S
Disney Cruise Ship. The Big Red Boat	$6.00	$4.50	$3.00	S
Disney, Princess Collection, Animated Princesses	$6.00	$4.50	$3.00	S
Disney, Various Characters, 1950s	$12.00	$9.00	$6.00	S
Disneyland	$4.00	$3.00	$2.00	S
Disneyland, Cinderella Castle	$5.00	$4.00	$2.50	S
Disneyland, Mini Deck, Various Designs	$3.00	$2.00	$1.50	M
Disney World	$4.00	$3.00	$2.00	S
Disney World, Cinderella Castle	$5.00	$4.00	$2.50	S
Disney World, Mini Deck	$3.00	$2.00	$1.50	M
Dr. Pepper, Soft Drink	$6.00	$4.50	$3.00	S
Dr. Pepper, Soft Drink, Girl Holding Bottle, 1946	$50.00	$40.00	$30.00	S
Dr. Van Dykes Holland Bitters, Bottle on Front, 1899			$150.00	S
Dodge Challenger	$6.00	$4.50	$3.00	S
Dodge Trucks, Lettering Only	$6.00	$4.50	$3.00	S
Dogs Playing Poker, 2 Deck Set in Tin	$10.00	$7.50	$5.00	DD
Dolly Madison, Bakery	$6.00	$4.50	$3.00	S
Dolly Madison, Quality Checked Selected Ice Cream	$4.00	$3.00	$2.00	S
Dolly Parton	$5.00	$4.00	$2.50	S
Dolphin Cruise Line, Cruise Ship	$6.00	$4.50	$3.00	S
Domino's Pizza, Avoid the Noid	$5.00	$4.00	$2.50	S
Domino's Pizza, Pizza Box	$5.00	$4.00	$2.50	S
Donald Duck, 1950s	$12.00	$9.00	$6.00	S
Dondorf #174, Swiss Face Cards, 1906		$100.00	$75.00	S
Dondorf #190, Patience Karten, Swiss Face Cards	$30.00	$25.00	$20.00	S
Dondorf Shakespeare #192, Gold Edges, Austria, 1920s			$150.00	S
Donkey Kong Junior, Ralston Cereal Premium	$8.00	$6.00	$4.00	S

Doral Cigarette	$6.00	$4.50	$3.00	S
Doritos Tortilla Chips	$6.00	$4.50	$3.00	S
Dorney Park, Allentown, PA	$4.00	$3.00	$2.00	S
Double Action, Diagonally Split Cards (2 on Each), 1 Joker, 1935		$50.00	$35.00	S
Dougherty Brand, New York, 1-Way Courts, No Indices, 1850s			$250.00	S
Dougherty Brand, 48-Card Tally-Ho Pinochle No.43			$25.00	S
Douglas DC-3–1937, Jet	$16.00	$12.00	$8.00	S
Douglas DC-4–1946, Jet	$16.00	$12.00	$8.00	S
Douglas DC-9–1966, Jet	$16.00	$12.00	$8.00	S
Dracula, Creepy Classics Oval Deck	$5.00	$4.00	$2.50	U
Drueke, Chess Knight Back	$8.00	$6.00	$4.00	S
Du Pont, Lettering Only	$4.00	$3.00	$2.00	S
Duke Blue Devils, University	$5.00	$4.00	$2.50	S
Duncan Hines, Cake Mix, 1951	$16.00	$12.00	$8.00	S
Dunkin Doughnuts	$10.00	$7.50	$5.00	S
Dunville's VR Whisky	$8.00	$6.00	$4.00	S
Duo Fast Tools	$1.00	$0.75	$0.50	S
Duracell Battery	$6.00	$4.50	$3.00	S
Durango & Silverton Narrow Gauge Railroad	$10.00	$7.50	$5.00	S
Duratone Brand, Velvet Case, 2-Deck Set, 1960s	$8.00	$6.00	$4.00	S
Dynastie Royale, Belgian Royalty Face Cards, 1934			$50.00	S
Early Times, Bottle of Bourbon, Just Mention My Name	$8.00	$6.00	$4.00	S
East Africa Wildlife Society, Nairobi, Kenya	$15.00	$11.00	$7.50	S
Easter Bunny & Bunny Shaped Cards in Tin, Fundex Games, 2002	$6.00	$4.50	$3.00	U
Easter Egg Tin & Egg-Shaped Cards, Fundex Games, 2002	$5.00	$4.00	$2.50	U
Eastern Airlines	$5.00	$4.00	$2.50	S
Eastern Airlines, Come Fly with Eastern	$5.00	$4.00	$2.50	S
Eastern State Penitentiary, Philadelphia, Pennsylvania	$2.00	$1.50	$1.00	S
Eastern Steamship Lines, Large Cruise Ship	$6.00	$4.50	$3.00	S
Eckerd Brand	$2.00	$1.50	$1.00	S
Edgewater Hotel & Casino	$2.00	$1.50	$1.00	S
Edison Mazda Light Bulbs, 1930	$350.00	$275.00	$200.00	S
Edmonton Oilers	$6.00	$4.50	$3.00	S
Edward Scissorhands, Movie, 1 Deck in Tin	$8.00	$6.00	$4.00	S
Edward VII & Alexandria Coronation, 1902			$100.00	S
Egyptian Playing Cards, Tourist Scenes	$4.00	$3.00	$2.00	S
8-Ball, Round Deck	$6.00	$4.50	$3.00	R
818 Poker Brand, Naipes, Spain	$3.00	$2.00	$1.00	S
El Cortez Hotel & Casino	$2.00	$1.50	$1.00	S
El Mirador Hotel, Palm Springs, California, 1960s	$5.00	$4.00	$2.50	S
El Navio, La Cubana, Spain, 1947			$35.00	S
Elsie, Borden Cow	$10.00	$7.50	$5.00	S
Elvis Presley, Best of, 54 Different Photos, 1 Each Card	$12.00	$9.00	$6.00	S
Elvis Presley, Many Varieties	$10.00	$7.50	$5.00	S
Elvis Presley, Piatnik of Austria Issue	$12.00	$9.00	$6.00	S
Empire State Building, New York	$4.00	$3.00	$2.00	S
English Ovals Cigarettes	$6.00	$4.50	$3.00	S
Enron Executive Crooks	$5.00	$4.00	$2.50	S
Epcot Center, Walt Disney World, Various Back Designs	$4.00	$3.00	$2.00	S
Erie Line, Railroad	$4.00	$3.00	$2.00	S
ESPN Magazine	$2.00	$1.50	$1.00	S
Europe, Tourist Deck, Cardboard Box	$4.00	$3.00	$2.00	S
Evinrude, Family in Boat, Miss Evinrude (Name of Boat)	$10.00	$7.50	$5.00	S
Evinrude, Man on Boat with Fish, Outboard Motor	$8.00	$6.00	$4.00	S
Evinrude, Outboard Motors	$6.00	$4.50	$3.00	S
Excalibur, Casino	$4.00	$3.00	$2.00	S
Excelsior Brand, Dougherty Co., No Indices, 1860			$500.00	S
Exportation Deck by I. Hardy, 1860s, 1-Face Cards, No Indices			$150.00	S
Exportation Deck by I. Hardy, 1980s Reproduction	$8.00	$6.00	$4.00	S
Falstaff Beer, Go Go Go For Falstaff, B&W Cartoon, 1940s	$20.00	$15.00	$10.00	S
Family Guy, Single Deck in Tin	$8.00	$6.00	$4.00	S
Farmers Insurance Group, Insurance Logo	$4.00	$3.00	$2.00	S
Faro, Spread Eagle, 1898			$500.00	S
Farrel Lines, African Route, Cruise Lines	$6.00	$4.50	$3.00	S
Farrel Lines, Africa Route, Double Deck Set, 1960	$30.00	$25.00	$20.00	DD
Felix the Cat, Several Varieties, Modern	$6.00	$4.50	$3.00	S
Ferris State College	$4.00	$3.00	$2.00	S
Fiesta Casino	$2.00	$1.50	$1.00	S
50 and Over, Humorous Double Deck Set on Aging, Plastic Case	$6.00	$4.50	$3.00	DD
Fire Food Specialties, Hot Sauce	$6.00	$4.50	$3.00	S
Firestone, The People Tire People, Double Deck Set	$10.00	$7.50	$5.00	DD
Firestone, Tires, Cut Your Tire Costs	$5.00	$4.00	$2.50	S
First National Bank	$3.00	$2.00	$1.50	S
Fitzgeralds, Casino	$2.00	$1.50	$1.00	S
562 Brand, Free Premium, Taiwan	$4.00	$3.00	$2.00	S
Flag Brand, Regular or Giant Face & Indices	$2.00	$1.50	$1.00	S
Flamingo, Casino	$2.00	$1.50	$1.00	S
Flamingo Capri Hotel & Casino	$2.00	$1.50	$1.00	S
Flamingo Hilton, Casino	$2.00	$1.50	$1.00	S
Fleischmann's Extra Dry Gin	$8.00	$6.00	$4.00	S
Fleischmann's Multi-Brand	$8.00	$6.00	$4.00	S
Flickers Photos of Movie Stars on each Card, 1974	$30.00	$22.50	$15.00	S
Florida E. Coast Souvenir, 1 Joker, 1920		$25.00	$15.00	S
Florida Gators, University	$5.00	$4.00	$2.50	S
Florida Marlins	$6.00	$4.50	$3.00	S
Florida Panthers	$6.00	$4.50	$3.00	S
Florida Souvenir, Various Scenes, Early 20th Century			$50.00	S
Florida State Seminoles, University	$5.00	$4.00	$2.50	S
Florsheim Shoes, The Florsheim Shoe	$4.00	$3.00	$2.00	S
Fluid King Pump Parts	$2.00	$1.50	$1.00	S
Flying Eagle Brand	$2.00	$1.50	$1.00	S
Flying Tiger Line	$16.00	$12.00	$8.00	S

Folklore, Piatnik, Double Deck Set	$12.00	$9.00	$6.00	DD
Fontana Dam, North Carolina	$4.00	$3.00	$2.00	S
Football Mini Deck, Oval Shaped	$2.00	$1.50	$1.00	M
Ford Construction Equipment, Front End Loader	$8.00	$6.00	$4.00	S
Ford GT, Gt Model Car, 1950s	$12.50	$10.00	$7.50	S
Ford Motor Company, Various Decks	$6.00	$4.50	$3.00	S
Ford Motor Company, 2-Deck Set in Tin	$10.00	$7.50	$5.00	DD
Ford MVP, 2 Deck Set in Box	$8.00	$6.00	$4.00	DD
Ford Tractor, 1940s Tractor	$8.00	$6.00	$4.00	S
Ford Tri-Motor—1929, Airplane	$16.00	$12.00	$8.00	S
Fort Howard Paper Co.	$2.00	$1.50	$1.00	S
Fort Robinson State Park	$2.00	$1.50	$1.00	S
Fortune Deck, 1896			$50.00	S
Four Queens, Casino	$2.00	$1.50	$1.00	S
Four Roses Distillery Double Set	$12.00	$9.00	$5.00	DD
Four Roses Whiskey	$6.00	$4.50	$3.00	S
Four Seasons, Austrian Face Cards, Piatnik, 1900		$75.00	$50.00	S
Fox Lake Brand, Norwood, Ohio	$1.50	$1.00	$0.75	S
France Royale, Piatnik, Double Deck Set	$12.00	$9.00	$6.00	DD
Frankenmuth, Michigan, Bavarian Scenery, Tourist	$4.00	$3.00	$2.00	S
Frankenstein, Creepy Classics Head-Shaped Deck	$5.00	$4.00	$2.50	U
Franklin Cigar, Ben Franklin, Gold Edges, 1 Joker, 1900			$100.00	S
Franklin National Life Insurance Company	$4.00	$3.00	$2.00	S
Fred Olsen Lines, Cruise Ship, Repeated on Opposite Side	$6.00	$4.50	$3.00	S
Freedom, Brand	$2.00	$1.50	$1.00	S
Fremont Hotel & Casino	$2.00	$1.50	$1.00	S
French Lick West Baden, Railroad	$8.00	$6.00	$4.00	S
French Line Railroad, 1925	$50.00	$40.00	$30.00	S
French, 2nd Empire Transformation Deck, 1860			$500.00	S
Frisco, Railroad, Double Deck Set	$10.00	$7.50	$5.00	DD
Frisco Line, Railroad	$8.00	$6.00	$4.00	S
Fritos Corn Chips	$6.00	$4.50	$3.00	S
Frontier Hotel & Casino	$2.00	$1.50	$1.00	S
Four Roses Premium, Whiskey	$8.00	$6.00	$4.00	S
Futurama, Cartoon, Double Deck Set in Tin	$12.00	$9.00	$6.00	DD
Gambler's Brand, Steamboat, 1932	$80.00	$60.00	$40.00	S
Game of Flags (Jeu de Drapeaux), French, Napoleon Honor, 1880s			$250.00	S
Gander Mountain, Outdoor Store	$6.00	$4.50	$3.00	S
Garfield the Cat, 2 Deck Set in Tin	$12.00	$9.00	$6.00	DD
Garfield the Cat, Various Decks	$5.00	$4.00	$2.50	S
Gateway Arch, St. Louis, Missouri	$4.00	$3.00	$2.00	S
Gatorade Thirst Quencher, Green or Orange Bottle Design	$6.00	$4.50	$3.00	S
Gemaco Brand	$1.50	$1.00	$0.50	S
Gemini the Twins, Zodiac Sign, 1960s	$10.00	$7.50	$5.00	S
General Dynamics	$10.00	$7.50	$5.00	S
General Electric Company	$4.00	$3.00	$2.00	S
General Electric Company, GE, Man-Made Diamond	$4.00	$3.00	$2.00	S
General Jackson, Paddlewheel Cruise Ship	$4.00	$3.00	$2.00	S
General Motors Parade of Progress, Bus & Ship	$4.00	$3.00	$2.00	S
General Motors, Various Decks	$4.00	$3.00	$2.00	S
George Killian's Irish Red, Beer	$10.00	$7.50	$5.00	S
Georgetown Hoyas, University	$5.00	$4.00	$2.50	S
Georgia Bulldogs, University	$5.00	$4.00	$2.50	S
Georgia R.R., Old Reliable 1834, Railroad	$6.00	$4.50	$3.00	S
Georgia State University	$4.00	$3.00	$2.00	S
Georgia Tech Hornets, University	$5.00	$4.00	$2.50	S
Gerber Baby Formula Modilac, Can with Classic Baby Head	$8.00	$6.00	$4.00	S
Gerber, Classic Baby Head in Circle, Double Deck Blue & Red Set	$16.00	$12.00	$8.00	S
Gettysburg National Military Park, Gettysburg, Pennsylvania	$5.00	$4.00	$2.50	S
GI Joe, Toy, Two Deck Set in Tin	$10.00	$7.50	$5.00	DD
Gilbey's London Dry Gin	$10.00	$7.50	$5.00	S
Gillette, Golden Horseshoe Club, 1959, Double Deck Set	$100.00	$75.00	$50.00	DD
Gladstone Brand by Russell, Various 2 Deck Sets in Holder	$2.00	$1.50	$1.00	DD
Glenlivit Whisky	$8.00	$6.00	$4.00	S
GM, Large letters, General Motors, Double Deck Set	$8.00	$6.00	$4.00	DD
GM & O Railroad	$6.00	$4.50	$3.00	S
Godzilla, Creepy Classics Oval Deck	$5.00	$4.00	$2.50	U
Gold Coast, Casino	$2.00	$1.50	$1.00	S
Gold River Gambling Hall & Resort	$2.00	$1.50	$1.00	S
Gold Spike Hotel & Casino	$2.00	$1.50	$1.00	S
Golden Class Brand, Finland	$2.00	$1.50	$1.00	S
Golden Gate, Casino	$2.00	$1.50	$1.00	S
Golden Gate Bridge, San Francisco	$4.00	$3.00	$2.00	S
Golden Lights Cigarettes	$6.00	$4.50	$3.00	S
Golden Nugget, Casino	$2.00	$1.50	$1.00	S
Golden State Warriors	$6.00	$4.50	$3.00	S
Gold Cartoons, 55-Card Deck by Piatnik	$5.00	$4.00	$2.50	S
Good Year, Name in Diamonds, Repeated on Opposite Side	$4.00	$3.00	$2.00	S
Goodrich Silvertowns, Repeated Once on Opposite Side (Tires)	$4.00	$3.00	$2.00	S
Gordon's London Dry Gin	$10.00	$7.50	$5.00	S
Gordon's London Dry Gin, Special Aces	$15.00	$10.00	$7.50	S
Graceland, Memphis, Tennessee, Mansion, Tourist, Plastic Case	$4.00	$3.00	$2.00	S
Grand Canyon National Park, Arizona	$4.00	$3.00	$2.00	S
Grand Hotel, Various Tourist Designs	$4.00	$3.00	$2.00	S
Grand Hotel, Horse & Buggy, Double Deck Set	$8.00	$6.00	$4.00	DD
Grand Hotel, Mackinac Island, MI, Various	$4.00	$3.00	$2.00	S
Grand Hotel, Mackinac Island, MI, Mini, Plastic Case	$3.00	$2.00	$1.50	M
Grand Imperial Gold Medals Brand, USPC, Wine Ad., 1900			$100.00	S
Grand Marnier Liquor	$10.00	$7.50	$5.00	S
Grand Ole Opry House, Nashville, Tennessee, Various	$3.00	$2.00	$1.50	S

Grand Teton National Park, Wyoming	$4.00	$3.00	$2.00	S
Grand Trunk Railroad Scene, 1905			$75.00	S
Grand Trunk Railway System	$8.00	$6.00	$4.00	S
Grant's Finest Scotch Whiskey	$10.00	$7.50	$5.00	S
Grateful Dead, Dancing Bears	$12.00	$9.00	$6.00	S
Grateful Dead, Skull in Circle, 1998	$8.00	$6.00	$4.00	S
Great Lakes Lighthouses, Tourist	$4.00	$3.00	$2.00	S
Great Lakes Ships, Tourist, Plastic Case	$4.00	$3.00	$2.00	S
Great Northern Railway	$8.00	$6.00	$4.00	S
Great Smoky Mountains, Bear	$1.00	$0.75	$0.50	S
Great Southwest, Indians on Horseback, 1901			$100.00	S
Greektown, Casino	$2.00	$1.50	$1.00	S
Green Bay Packers	$6.00	$4.50	$3.00	S
Greenfield Village	$4.00	$3.00	$2.00	S
Guckenheimer American Whiskey	$8.00	$6.00	$4.00	S
Guinness Extra Stout, Beer	$8.00	$6.00	$4.00	S
Gulf, Be a Winner, Indy '500' Souvenir	$6.00	$4.50	$3.00	S
Gulf Oil, Orange Logo	$8.00	$6.00	$4.00	S
Gulf Research Center, Building with Gulf Oil Sign	$6.00	$4.50	$3.00	S
Gypsy Witch Fortune Telling, Cardboard Case	$30.00	$22.50	$15.00	S
Hacienda, Casino	$2.00	$1.50	$1.00	S
Hager, Everything Hinges on Hager	$4.00	$3.00	$2.00	S
Haggar Slacks, Dallas	$5.00	$4.00	$2.50	S
Haig Blended Scotch Whiskey	$10.00	$7.50	$5.00	S
Hallmark Cigarettes	$6.00	$4.50	$3.00	S
Halloween 2006, Cat Face Shaped Deck	$2.00	$1.50	$1.00	U
Halloween 2006, Pumpkin (Jack-O-Lantern) Shaped Deck	$2.00	$1.50	$1.00	U
Halloween 2006, Candy Corn Face Shaped Deck	$2.00	$1.50	$1.00	U
Hamart Promotions	$6.00	$4.50	$3.00	S
Hamilton Brand, 48-Card Pinochle Deck, 1950s	$6.00	$4.50	$3.00	P
Hamm's Beer, Land of Sky Blue Waters, Special Aces, 1950s	$40.00	$30.00	$20.00	S
Hamm's Beer, Man, Bear, River Scene	$10.00	$7.50	$5.00	S
Handy Helpful Hints, Hoyle	$3.00	$2.00	$1.50	S
Hanzel, Blue Spades, Yellow Diamonds, Green Clubs; 1925			$150.00	S
Happy Bunny, Humorous	$6.00	$4.50	$3.00	S
Happy Chef	$2.00	$1.50	$1.00	S
Hard Rock Hotel & Casino	$2.00	$1.50	$1.00	S
Harlequin, Tiffany Transformation, Carryl, Red Backs, 1879			$2,500	S
Harley Davidson Cigarettes	$6.00	$4.50	$3.00	S
Harley Davidson, Motorcycles, Double Deck Set in Tin	$12.00	$9.00	$6.00	DD
Harley Davidson Motorcycles, Various Modern Deck Designs	$6.00	$4.50	$3.00	S
Harold's or Harold's Club, Casino	$2.00	$1.50	$1.00	S
Harrah's, Casino	$2.00	$1.50	$1.00	S
Harry Potter	$5.00	$4.00	$2.50	S
Harry Potter, Round Deck in Tin	$8.00	$6.00	$4.00	R
Hartford Whalers	$6.00	$4.50	$3.00	S
Hawaii, Tourist, Various Designs	$4.00	$3.00	$2.00	S
Hearst Castle, San Simeon, California	$4.00	$3.00	$2.00	S
Heart Shaped Deck, Mini	$2.00	$1.50	$1.00	U
Heineken Beer	$8.00	$6.00	$4.00	S
Heinz Catsup	$10.00	$7.50	$5.00	S
Hell, Michigan, Souvenir	$4.00	$3.00	$2.00	S
Hello Kitty, 2000	$8.00	$6.00	$4.00	S
Hennessy Cognac	$10.00	$7.50	$5.00	S
Henry Ford Museum	$4.00	$3.00	$2.00	S
Hershey's Chocolate Bar	$4.00	$3.00	$2.00	S
Hershey's Chocolate World, Mini Deck, Plastic Case	$3.00	$2.00	$1.50	M
Hershey's Grandma & Grandpa Chefs, 2-Deck Set, 1970s	$10.00	$7.50	$5.00	DD
Hershey's Milk Chocolate Kisses, Girl Feeding Boy	$8.00	$6.00	$4.00	S
Hershey's Syrup, Can Design, 1960s	$15.00	$11.50	$7.50	S
Hertz Rent A Car	$6.00	$4.50	$3.00	S
Hertz Rent A Car, Large Globe, Double Deck Set	$10.00	$7.50	$5.00	DD
Hickory Farms, Antique Car, Barn and Two Silos	$8.00	$6.00	$4.00	S
Hickory Farms on Mail Box, Barn and Two Silos	$8.00	$6.00	$4.00	S
Highland Queen Scotch Whiskey	$10.00	$7.50	$5.00	S
Highlanders Brand, Scottish Highlander, 1-Way Face Cards, 1864			$350.00	S
Highlanders Brand, Scottish Highlander, 1998 Reproduction Deck	$6.00	$4.50	$3.00	S
Hilton Hotel & Casino	$2.00	$1.50	$1.00	S
Hiram Walker Bourbon Whiskey	$8.00	$6.00	$4.00	S
Hiram Walker Peppermint Schnapps	$8.00	$6.00	$4.00	S
Hires Root Beer, Pin-Up Girl, Clothed, 1950s	$16.00	$12.00	$8.00	S
Hispania, Piatnik, Double Deck Set	$12.00	$9.00	$6.00	DD
Holiday Casino	$2.00	$1.50	$1.00	S
Holiday Inn, Free Standing Sign Design	$10.00	$7.50	$5.00	S
Holland American Lines, Cruise Ship, Repeated on Opp. Side	$6.00	$4.50	$3.00	S
Holland American Lines, Boat in Oval, Repeated on Opp. Side	$6.00	$4.50	$3.00	S
Holland House, Whiskey	$8.00	$6.00	$4.00	S
Holland, Tourist, Windmills & Tulips, Made in Holland, Cardboard Box	$5.00	$4.00	$2.50	S
Hollywood Sign, California Tourist, Cardboard Box	$4.00	$3.00	$2.00	S
Honda Motorcycles, 1970s	$6.00	$4.50	$3.00	S
Hong Kong Bridge & Castle, Tourist, 1960s	$5.00	$4.00	$2.50	S
Hong Kong Round Cards, Plastic Case, 1960s	$6.00	$4.50	$3.00	U
Hooters Models, 1997	$10.00	$7.50	$5.00	S
Hoover Dam, Nevada/Arizona Border	$4.00	$3.00	$2.00	S
Horseshoe or Horseshoe Club Casino	$2.00	$1.50	$1.00	S
Hot Point All-Electric Kitchen '50s Kitchen Scene	$8.00	$6.00	$4.00	S
Hot Point Automatic Home Laundry, Washer & Dryer	$6.00	$4.50	$3.00	S
Hot Point Automatic Home Laundry, '50s Laundry Room	$8.00	$6.00	$4.00	S
Hot Springs National Park	$4.00	$3.00	$2.00	S
Hot Wheels Cars, Toys, Various Backs	$6.00	$4.50	$3.00	S
Hot Wheels Cars, Toys, Double Deck Set in Tin	$12.00	$9.00	$6.00	DD

Hotel Jefferson, Hotel Building	$6.00	$4.50	$3.00	S
Hotel Nevada, Casino	$2.00	$1.50	$1.00	S
Houston Astros	$6.00	$4.50	$3.00	S
Houston Oilers	$8.00	$6.00	$4.00	S
Houston Rockets	$6.00	$4.50	$3.00	S
Houston, Texans	$6.00	$4.50	$3.00	S
Hovis Bread by Waddingtons, 1890s			$100.00	S
Hoyle Brand	$1.50	$1.00	$0.75	S
Hoyle Brand, Double Deck Set in Plastic Case, Various Designs	$5.00	$4.00	$2.50	DD
Hoyle Brand—48-Card Pinochle Deck	$1.50	$1.00	$0.75	P
Huber Brewing Company	$8.00	$6.00	$4.00	S
Hulk, 2004	$4.00	$3.00	$2.00	S
Hundred Dollar Bill Design, U.S., Ben Franklin	$4.00	$3.00	$2.00	S
Hungaria, Piatnik, Double Deck Set	$12.00	$9.00	$6.00	DD
Hunt & Sons, England, One-Way Face Cards, No Indices, 1830s			$250.00	S
Hustling Joe Brand, USPC, Transformation, 1 Joker, 1895			$750.00	S
IBM Quarter Century Club	$1.00	$0.75	$0.50	S
Ice Capades, Female Skater, 1960s	$8.00	$6.00	$4.00	S
Idaho, Potato, Tourist	$4.00	$3.00	$2.00	S
Ideal Electric Company	$3.00	$2.00	$1.50	S
Illinois Central, Railroad	$6.00	$4.50	$3.00	S
Illinois State Outline	$1.00	$0.75	$0.50	S
Illusions, Y&B Associates, Double Deck Set, 1987	$10.00	$7.50	$5.00	DD
Imperial Brand	$2.00	$1.50	$1.00	S
Imperial Vodka	$10.00	$7.50	$5.00	S
Inca Dynasty, Peru Tourist	$2.00	$1.50	$1.00	S
Inca Indian, Brown & Bigelow, 1948		$50.00	$35.00	S
Incredible Hulk, Motion Picture	$6.00	$4.50	$3.00	S
The Incredibles, Animated Film, 2004	$6.00	$4.50	$3.00	S
Independence Hall	$1.00	$0.75	$0.50	S
Indiana Hoosiers, University	$5.00	$4.00	$2.50	S
Indiana Jones, Double Deck Movie Set (all 4 movies represented)	$10.00	$7.50	$5.00	DD
Indiana Pacers	$6.00	$4.50	$3.00	S
Indianapolis Colts	$6.00	$4.50	$3.00	S
Indianapolis Motor Speedway, Winged Tire & Flags, 500-Mile Race	$8.00	$6.00	$4.00	S
Instant Cash	$1.00	$0.75	$0.50	S
Intel Fax Modem 1.44	$6.00	$4.50	$3.00	S
Inter-Mountain Railroad, 1910s		$50.00	$35.00	S
Invincible Brand #303 48-Card Pinochle, 1940s–1950s	$4.00	$3.00	$2.00	S
Iowa, Cornfield, Tourist	$4.00	$3.00	$2.00	S
Iowa, Farm Scene, Mini Deck, Plastic Case	$3.00	$2.00	$1.50	M
Iowa Hawkeyes, University	$5.00	$4.00	$2.50	S
Iraq, Most Wanted Deck	$4.00	$3.00	$2.00	S
Ireland, Find Ireland	$1.00	$0.75	$0.50	S
J & B Scotch Whiskey	$10.00	$7.50	$5.00	S
Jack Daniels, No.7 Brand Logo, Whiskey, Various Styles	$8.00	$6.00	$4.00	S
Jack Daniels, 2 Deck Set in Tin	$16.00	$12.00	$8.00	DD
Jack Daniels, Unique Design on Face Cards, 1970	$12.00	$9.00	$6.00	S
Jack Daniels, Whiskey, Various Styles	$8.00	$6.00	$4.00	S
Jackson Hole, Wyoming, Tourist	$4.00	$3.00	$2.00	S
Jacksonville Jaguars	$6.00	$4.50	$3.00	S
Jaeger Equipment, Cranes & Construction Scene	$8.00	$6.00	$4.00	S
James Bond 007, 40th Anniversary 1962–2002, 2 Deck Set in Tin	$16.00	$12.00	$8.00	DD
Jameson Irish Whiskey	$8.00	$6.00	$4.00	S
Japan Air Lines, Symbols in Squares	$8.00	$6.00	$4.00	S
JC Penney	$6.00	$4.50	$3.00	S
Jefferson Standard Life Insurance Co., Building	$4.00	$3.00	$2.00	S
Jerry's Nugget, North Las Vegas, Casino	$2.00	$1.50	$1.00	S
Jersey Whiskey, 1902			$75.00	S
Jim Beam, Bourbon	$8.00	$6.00	$4.00	S
Jim Beam, 2-Deck Set in Tin	$16.00	$12.00	$8.00	DD
Joan of Arc, Merrimack, 1965	$10.00	$7.50	$5.00	S
Joe's Crab Shack	$4.00	$3.00	$2.00	S
John Ascuaga's Nugget, Casino	$2.00	$1.50	$1.00	S
John Deere, Various Company Logos	$6.00	$4.50	$3.00	S
John Deere, Logo, Nothing Runs Like a Deere Repeated	$8.00	$6.00	$4.00	S
John Deere, Large Tractor	$8.00	$6.00	$4.00	S
John Power & Son Dublin Whiskey	$10.00	$7.50	$5.00	S
John Wayne American Legend, 2 Deck Set in Tin	$12.00	$9.00	$6.00	DD
Johnnie Walker Black Label Scotch	$8.00	$6.00	$4.00	S
Johnnie Walker Red, Man Walking	$6.00	$4.50	$3.00	S
Johnson Outboard Motors, Double Deck Set, 1951	$50.00	$40.00	$30.00	DD
JoyTyme Brand, Oleet Playing Card Co., Red Presentation Box	$4.00	$3.00	$2.00	S
Judge Brand, Easy Flips, 48-Card Pinochle Deck, 1950s	$6.00	$4.50	$3.00	P
Jumbo Brand Playing Cards	$2.00	$1.50	$1.00	S
Jurassic Park, Motion Picture	$12.00	$9.00	$6.00	S
Kaiser, Piatnik, Double Deck Set	$12.00	$9.00	$6.00	DD
Kansas, Sunflower	$4.00	$3.00	$2.00	S
Kansas City Chiefs	$6.00	$4.50	$3.00	S
Kansas City International Airport	$2.00	$1.50	$1.00	S
Kansas City Royals	$6.00	$4.50	$3.00	S
Kansas City Southern Lines, Railroad	$8.00	$6.00	$4.00	S
Kansas City Southern Lines, Railroad, Double Deck Set	$16.00	$12.00	$8.00	DD
Kansas State Wildcats, University	$5.00	$4.00	$2.50	S
KATY Lines, Railroad	$8.00	$6.00	$4.00	S
Kay Jewelers, Coast to Coast, Double Deck Set	$6.00	$4.50	$3.00	DD
Kellogg's Cereal, 1994	$4.00	$3.00	$2.00	S
Kellogg's Frosties, Tony the Tiger (British Version of Frosted Flakes)	$8.00	$6.00	$4.00	S
Kelly Tires, Lettering Only	$3.00	$2.00	$1.50	S
Kem Co. Playing Cards, Unique Ace of Spades, Leaf Backs, 1935	$40.00	$30.00	$20.00	S
Kenmore Turbo-matic Washer & Dryer, Sears, 1960s	$6.00	$4.50	$3.00	S
Kennedy Kards (JFK Caricature Face Cards), Humor House, 1963	$40.00	$30.00	$20.00	S
Kennedy Space Center	$4.00	$3.00	$2.00	S
Kenny Rogers, Jax Ltd., 1981	$8.00	$6.00	$4.00	S
Kent Cigarettes, Chess Pieces	$8.00	$6.00	$4.00	S

Kent Cigarettes, Pack Design, Various Styles	$6.00	$4.50	$3.00	S
Kentucky Derby, Dated & Numbered for Each Year, 1970s–Up	$8.00	$6.00	$4.00	S
Kentucky Fried Chicken, Repeated Colonel Sanders Logo, 1976	$12.00	$9.00	$6.00	S
Kentucky Waldorf Playing Cards #230, 1920s			$40.00	S
Kentucky Wildcats, University	$5.00	$4.00	$2.50	S
Kessler Whiskey	$6.00	$4.50	$3.00	S
Killark Electric	$1.00	$0.75	$0.50	S
Killington, Vermont, Tourist (Ski Resort)	$4.00	$3.00	$2.00	S
King George VI & Queen Elizabeth, Double Deck Set	$40.00	$30.00	$20.00	DD
King Kong, Creepy Classics Oval Deck	$5.00	$4.00	$2.50	U
Kings Island, Amusement Park	$4.00	$3.00	$2.00	S
Kingsir Brand	$1.00	$0.75	$0.50	S
Kis-Me Cooks, Pepsin	$2.00	$1.50	$1.00	S
KLM Air	$8.00	$6.00	$4.00	S
Knights of Camelot, Wood Box w. Fabric Cover, DD Set, Hong Kong, 1960s	$16.00	$12.00	$8.00	DD
Knotts Berry Farm	$4.00	$3.00	$2.00	S
Knox Unflavored Gelatine, Get to Know Knox The Real Gelatine	$4.00	$3.00	$2.00	S
Kool or Kool Milds Cigarettes, Various	$6.00	$4.50	$3.00	S
Kool-Aid	$10.00	$7.50	$5.00	S
Korean Air Lines, Jet in Flight	$5.00	$4.00	$2.50	S
L & A The Better Way Railway	$6.00	$4.50	$3.00	S
L & M Oilfield Equipment	$6.00	$4.50	$3.00	S
L & N, Railroad	$6.00	$4.50	$3.00	S
L & N, Railroad, 6 Different Block Scenes on Back	$10.00	$7.50	$5.00	S
La Cage, Riviera, Stage Show	$3.00	$2.00	$1.50	S
Lackawanna Railroad, Red & White Line (rare)	$100.00	$75.00	$50.00	S
Lady, Piatnik, Double Deck Set	$12.00	$9.00	$6.00	DD
Lamb's Navy Rum	$10.00	$7.50	$5.00	S
Las Vegas, 100-Year Anniversary, 2-Deck Set	$8.00	$6.00	$4.00	DD
Las Vegas, Strip, Tourist, Various Designs	$3.00	$2.00	$1.50	S
Las Vegas Club, Casino	$2.00	$1.50	$1.00	S
Laugh-In Television Show, 1969	$10.00	$7.50	$5.00	S
Lays Potato Chips	$6.00	$4.50	$3.00	S
LBJ, The Texas White House (LBJ's Home)	$4.00	$3.00	$2.00	S
League, Red, 1920			$75.00	S
Lehigh Valley Railroad	$4.00	$3.00	$2.00	S
Lemon Hart Golden Jamaica Rum	$10.00	$7.50	$5.00	S
Lenox, Tools in the Plaid Box	$4.00	$3.00	$2.00	S
Leo the Lion, Zodiac Sign, 1960s	$10.00	$7.50	$5.00	S
Levi Strauss, Jeans Logo	$10.00	$7.50	$5.00	S
Lewis & Clark, 200th Anniversary, 2004	$3.00	$2.00	$1.50	S
Libra the Balance, Zodiac Sign, 1960s	$10.00	$7.50	$5.00	S
Life Savers, 36 Rolls	$10.00	$7.50	$5.00	S
Lincoln Iron & Steel Co.	$4.00	$3.00	$2.00	S
Lincoln National Life Insurance Company, Abe Lincoln Bust	$6.00	$4.50	$3.00	S
Lion King, Animated Disney Film, 1990s	$8.00	$6.00	$4.00	S
Lisa Frank Toy Series Playing Cards	$4.00	$3.00	$2.00	S
Lite Beer, Miller, Lettering Only	$6.00	$4.50	$3.00	S
Lite Beer, Miller, Various Logo Designs	$8.00	$6.00	$4.00	S
Little Dukes Toy Cards, #24 Double Mini Set in Leather Holder	$8.00	$6.00	$4.00	DD
Lockheed 749—1950, Jet	$16.00	$12.00	$8.00	S
Lockheed 1049—1952, Jet	$16.00	$12.00	$8.00	S
Lockheed 1049G—1955, Jet	$16.00	$12.00	$8.00	S
Lockheed 1649—1957, Jet	$16.00	$12.00	$8.00	S
London Guard on Deck and Tin, England	$6.00	$4.50	$3.00	S
Lone Star Beer, Logo	$8.00	$6.00	$4.00	S
Long John Scotch Whiskey	$10.00	$7.50	$5.00	S
Longfellow & Emerson Homes, Congress, Double Deck Set, 1950s	$30.00	$25.00	$20.00	S
Looney Tunes, 4-Squares, Various Characters, 1990s	$8.00	$6.00	$4.00	S
Looney Tunes Mini Deck, Various Characters	$4.00	$3.00	$2.00	M
Lord of the Rings	$10.00	$7.50	$5.00	S
Los Angeles Clippers	$6.00	$4.50	$3.00	S
Los Angeles Dodgers	$6.00	$4.50	$3.00	S
Los Angeles Kings	$6.00	$4.50	$3.00	S
Los Angeles Lakers	$6.00	$4.50	$3.00	S
Los Angeles, Olympics, 1984	$5.00	$4.00	$2.50	S
Los Angeles Raiders	$6.00	$4.50	$3.00	S
Los Angeles Rams	$6.00	$4.50	$3.00	S
Louis XV, Grimaud France, French Face Cards, 1890			$125.00	S
Louisville Cardinals, University	$5.00	$4.00	$2.50	S
Love Boat, Cruise Ship, Princess Cruises	$5.00	$4.00	$2.50	S
Love Stamp, 20-Cents, U.S. Postal Service	$6.00	$4.50	$3.00	S
Luden's Wild Cherry Cough Drops, Box Design, 1950s	$12.00	$9.00	$6.00	S
Lummi, Casino	$2.00	$1.50	$1.00	S
Luxor, Casino	$2.00	$1.50	$1.00	S
Luxury, Piatnik, Double Deck Set	$12.00	$9.00	$6.00	DD
M & M's, Various Back Designs, 1990s	$8.00	$6.00	$4.00	S
Mackenzie Premium Scotch	$10.00	$7.50	$5.00	S
Mackinac Bridge, Michigan, Cardboard Box	$4.00	$3.00	$2.00	S
Mackinac Bridge, Michigan, Mini Deck	$1.00	$0.75	$0.50	M
Mackinac Island, Michigan	$4.00	$3.00	$2.00	S
Mackinac Island, Michigan, Mini Deck, Plastic Case	$3.00	$2.00	$1.50	M
Maine Lighthouses, Tourist, Cardboard Box	$4.00	$3.00	$2.00	S
Maine Lobster, Tourist	$4.00	$3.00	$2.00	S
Malaysia, Dolphin Brand	$1.00	$0.75	$0.50	S
Mall of America, Minnesota, Tourist	$4.00	$3.00	$2.00	S
Mallard Ducks, KEM, Double Deck Set in Plastic Case	$14.00	$10.50	$7.00	DD
Mammoth Cave, Kentucky	$4.00	$3.00	$2.00	S
Man from U.N.C.L.E., TV Series, 1960s	$10.00	$7.50	$5.00	S
Manchester Liners, ML in Flag, Repeated on Opposite Side	$6.00	$4.50	$3.00	S
Mandalay Bay Hotel & Casino	$2.00	$1.50	$1.00	S
Manufacturer's Railroad	$6.00	$4.50	$3.00	S
Mao Zedong, Work is Struggling	$6.00	$4.50	$3.00	S
Marathon Oil Company	$6.00	$4.50	$3.00	S
Marathon, The Ohio Oil Company	$4.00	$3.00	$2.00	S
Mardi Gras, Cruise the Fun				

Ship, Cruise Lines	$6.00	$4.50	$3.00	S
Marilyn Monroe, Bathing Suit, 1950s	$60.00	$45.00	$30.00	S
Marilyn Monroe, Nude, 1950s, Tom Kelley's "A New Wrinkle" Pose	$80.00	$60.00	$40.00	S
Marilyn Monroe, Nude, 1950s, Tom Kelley's "Golden Dream" Pose	$80.00	$60.00	$40.00	S
Marilyn Monroe, Nude, 1950s Double Deck Set (Tom Kelley poses)	$200.00	$150.00	$100.00	DD
Marilyn Monroe, Portrait, Bicycle, Various New Releases	$6.00	$4.50	$3.00	S
Marlboro Cigarettes, Marlboro Man	$8.00	$6.00	$4.00	S
Marlboro Cigarettes, Marlboro Man, Double Deck Set	$20.00	$15.00	$10.00	DD
Marlboro Cigarettes, Pack Design	$6.00	$4.50	$3.00	S
Marriott Hotels	$6.00	$4.50	$3.00	S
Martha Stewart, Her & Associates on Face Cards	$6.00	$4.50	$3.00	S
Martin 404—1950, Jet	$16.00	$12.00	$8.00	S
Mary Engelbreit, Artist, Double Deck Set	$12.00	$9.00	$6.00	DD
Maryland and Pennsylvania Railroad	$4.00	$3.00	$2.00	S
Maryland is for Crabs, Crabs	$4.00	$3.00	$2.00	S
M*A*S*H 4077th, 1970, 1981 Twentieth Century Fox	$10.00	$7.50	$5.00	S
Massenghini Circus, Italy, 1975	$20.00	$15.00	$10.00	S
Maui, Hawaii, Tourist	$4.00	$3.00	$2.00	S
Maverick Brand, Horse Backs	$1.50	$1.00	$0.50	S
Maverick Brand, 48-Card Pinochle Deck	$1.50	$1.00	$0.50	P
Maverick Brand, Revolver on Deck, Small Stamp—1940	$20.00	$15.00	$10.00	S
Maxine, Cartoon Character, Hallmark	$4.00	$3.00	$2.00	S
Maxine, Cartoon Character, Hallmark, Double Deck Set	$8.00	$6.00	$4.00	DD
Mayflower, Moving Company	$4.00	$3.00	$2.00	S
McDonald's, Restaurant, 1970s	$16.00	$12.00	$8.00	S
Memphis Grizzlies	$6.00	$4.50	$3.00	S
Meramac Caverns, Missouri	$4.00	$3.00	$2.00	S
Merit Cigarettes	$6.00	$4.50	$3.00	S
Merryl Lynch, Bull & Jet Icons, Plastic Case	$6.00	$4.50	$3.00	S
Metropolitan Museum of Art	$4.00	$3.00	$2.00	S
MGM Grand Casino	$2.00	$1.50	$1.00	S
MGS Embossed Brand, Kajyuan Printing, Taiwan	$2.00	$1.50	$1.00	S
Miami Dolphins	$6.00	$4.50	$3.00	S
Miami Heat	$6.00	$4.50	$3.00	S
Miami Hurricanes, University	$5.00	$4.00	$2.50	S
Michelin, Repeated in Tire Pattern	$8.00	$6.00	$4.00	S
Michelin Man, Tires	$12.00	$9.00	$6.00	S
Michelob Beer, Logo	$8.00	$6.00	$4.00	S
Michelob Beer, Double Deck Set	$16.00	$12.00	$8.00	DD
Michigan Cherry Festival	$1.00	$0.75	$0.50	S
Michigan Lighthouses, Cardboard Box	$4.00	$3.00	$2.00	S
Michigan Lottery	$2.00	$1.50	$1.00	S
Michigan State Police	$5.00	$4.00	$2.50	S
Michigan State Spartans, University	$5.00	$4.00	$2.50	S
Michigan Upper Peninsula, Tourist	$4.00	$3.00	$2.00	S
Michigan Wildflowers, Tourist	$4.00	$3.00	$2.00	S
Michigan Wolverines, University	$5.00	$4.00	$2.50	S
Mickey Mouse, Disney, Double Deck 75th Anniversary Set in Tin	$12.00	$9.00	$6.00	DD
Mickey Mouse, Disney, Modern	$8.00	$6.00	$4.00	S
Mickey Mouse, Disney, 1950s	$12.00	$9.00	$6.00	S
Miller Genuine Draft, Beer	$6.00	$4.50	$3.00	S
Miller High Life Beer, Writing Only	$6.00	$4.50	$3.00	S
Miller High Life Beer, Logo	$8.00	$6.00	$4.00	S
Miller High Life Beer, Double Deck Set	$16.00	$12.00	$8.00	DD
Milwaukee Brewers	$6.00	$4.50	$3.00	S
Milwaukee Bucks	$6.00	$4.50	$3.00	S
Milwaukee Clipper, Large Cruise Ship	$6.00	$4.50	$3.00	S
The Milwaukee Road, Railroad	$6.00	$4.50	$3.00	S
Minnesota Golden Gophers, University	$5.00	$4.00	$2.50	S
Minnesota North Stars	$8.00	$6.00	$4.00	S
Minnesota State Outline	$1.00	$0.75	$0.50	S
Minnesota Timberwolves	$6.00	$4.50	$3.00	S
Minnesota Twins	$6.00	$4.50	$3.00	S
Minnesota Vikings	$6.00	$4.50	$3.00	S
Minnesota Wild	$6.00	$4.50	$3.00	S
The Mint Hotel & Casino	$2.00	$1.50	$1.00	S
The Mirador Hotel, Palm Springs, California	$6.00	$4.50	$3.00	S
Mirage, Casino	$2.00	$1.50	$1.00	S
Miss World, Nude Face Cards, 1950	$20.00	$15.00	$10.00	S
Mississippi Riverboat, Paddlewheeler	$6.00	$4.50	$3.00	S
Missouri Double Deck Tourist Set	$3.00	$2.00	$1.50	DD
Missouri Pacific Lines, Railroad	$6.00	$4.50	$3.00	S
Mr. Potato Head, Characters on all Cards, Large Size Deck	$12.00	$9.00	$6.00	U
MLB, Round Baseball Deck, Cardboard Box	$6.00	$4.50	$3.00	R
Mobil Gas	$6.00	$4.50	$3.00	S
Mobil Oil, Lettering Only	$4.00	$3.00	$2.00	S
Mobil Oil, Red Pegasus Logo	$20.00	$15.00	$10.00	S
Mobil Packaging Coatings	$4.00	$3.00	$2.00	S
Moller Steamship Co.—Maersk Line, Double Deck Set	$30.00	$25.00	$20.00	DD
Monet Gallery, Double Art Deck, Lilac Garden Cover, Piatnik	$16.00	$12.00	$8.00	DD
Monet Gallery, Double Art Deck, Water Lilies Cover, Piatnik	$16.00	$12.00	$8.00	DD
Monon The Hoosier Line, Railroad	$6.00	$4.50	$3.00	S
Monopole Champagne	$8.00	$6.00	$4.00	S
Monroe, Auto Parts, Congress, 2-Deck Set in Velvet Box, 1960s	$12.00	$9.00	$6.00	DD
Monsters, Inc., Animated Film, Fuzzy Furry Spotted Case	$12.00	$9.00	$6.00	U
Monsters, Inc., Animated Film, Round "EYE" Deck	$10.00	$7.50	$5.00	S
Montclair WW II Planes	$16.00	$12.00	$8.00	S
Monte Carlo, Casino	$2.00	$1.50	$1.00	S
Montreal Canadiens	$6.00	$4.50	$3.00	S
Montreal Expos	$6.00	$4.50	$3.00	S
Moore McCormick Lines, Cruise Ship	$6.00	$4.50	$3.00	S
Mo-Pac, Railroad	$6.00	$4.50	$3.00	S
More Cigarette	$6.00	$4.50	$3.00	S
Mother's Best Flower, 1951	$12.00	$8.00	$6.00	S
Mott Bros. Company	$3.00	$2.00	$1.50	S
Mount Rushmore, South Dakota	$4.00	$3.00	$2.00	S

Mountain Dew, Various Deck Designs	$6.00	$4.50	$3.00	S
Movie Set, Antique Souvenir, 1920s		$120.00	$80.00	S
Mummy, Creepy Classics Oval Deck	$5.00	$4.00	$2.50	U
Muppet Show, TV Show, 2 Deck Set in Tin	$12.00	$9.00	$6.00	DD
Murphy Varnish, Transformation Deck, 1883			$3,500	S
Murphy's Oil Soap	$10.00	$7.50	$5.00	S
Muzak, Music by Muzak	$4.00	$3.00	$2.00	S
Myrtle Beach, Beach Scene, South Carolina	$4.00	$3.00	$2.00	S
Mystic Seaport, Connecticut	$4.00	$3.00	$2.00	S
Nabisco Thing	$6.00	$4.50	$3.00	S
Napoleon III, 2nd Empire	$5.00	$4.00	$2.50	S
Narragansett Lager Beer	$5.00	$4.00	$2.50	S
NASA, Johnson Space Center, Houston, Texas	$8.00	$6.00	$4.00	S
NASCAR, Bill Elliott	$8.00	$6.00	$4.00	S
NASCAR, Bobby Hamilton	$8.00	$6.00	$4.00	S
NASCAR, Bobby Labonte	$8.00	$6.00	$4.00	S
NASCAR Café	$6.00	$4.50	$3.00	S
NASCAR, Chad Little	$8.00	$6.00	$4.00	S
NASCAR, Coca-Cola Team	$8.00	$6.00	$4.00	S
NASCAR Collector Series, 1947–1959	$8.00	$6.00	$4.00	S
NASCAR, Dale Earnhardt, The Intimidator	$12.00	$9.00	$6.00	S
NASCAR, Dale Earnhardt, Commemorative 2 Deck Set in Tin	$25.00	$17.50	$12.50	DD
NASCAR, Dale Earnhardt Jr.	$8.00	$6.00	$4.00	S
NASCAR, Dale Jarrett	$8.00	$6.00	$4.00	S
NASCAR, Davy Allison	$8.00	$6.00	$4.00	S
NASCAR, Elliott Sadler	$8.00	$6.00	$4.00	S
NASCAR, Ernie Irvan	$8.00	$6.00	$4.00	S
NASCAR, 50th Anniversary	$8.00	$6.00	$4.00	S
NASCAR, Geoff Bodine	$8.00	$6.00	$4.00	S
NASCAR, Jeff Burton	$8.00	$6.00	$4.00	S
NASCAR, Jeff Gordon	$8.00	$6.00	$4.00	S
NASCAR, Jeremy Mayfield	$8.00	$6.00	$4.00	S
NASCAR, Jimmy Johnson	$8.00	$6.00	$4.00	S
NASCAR, Johnny Benson	$8.00	$6.00	$4.00	S
NASCAR, Harry Gant	$8.00	$6.00	$4.00	S
NASCAR, Ken Schrade	$8.00	$6.00	$4.00	S
NASCAR, Kevin Harvick	$8.00	$6.00	$4.00	S
NASCAR, Kurt Busch	$8.00	$6.00	$4.00	S
NASCAR, Kyle Petty	$8.00	$6.00	$4.00	S
NASCAR, Logo	$4.00	$3.00	$2.00	U
NASCAR, Mark Martin	$8.00	$6.00	$4.00	S
NASCAR, Matt Kenseth	$8.00	$6.00	$4.00	S
NASCAR, Maxwell House #22 Ford Thunderbird	$8.00	$6.00	$4.00	S
NASCAR, Michael Waltrip	$8.00	$6.00	$4.00	S
NASCAR, Ricky Rudd	$8.00	$6.00	$4.00	S
NASCAR, Richard Petty	$10.00	$7.50	$5.00	S
NASCAR, Roush Racing	$8.00	$6.00	$4.00	S
NASCAR, Rusty Wallace	$8.00	$6.00	$4.00	S
NASCAR, Ryan Newman	$8.00	$6.00	$4.00	S
NASCAR, Sterling Martin	$8.00	$6.00	$4.00	S
NASCAR, Steve Kinser	$8.00	$6.00	$4.00	S
NASCAR, Steve Parks	$8.00	$6.00	$4.00	S
NASCAR, Tony Stewart	$8.00	$6.00	$4.00	S
Nashville Predators	$6.00	$4.50	$3.00	S
Nashville Zoo, Tennessee, Tourist, Plastic Case	$4.00	$3.00	$2.00	S
National Air & Space Museum, Washington DC	$4.00	$3.00	$2.00	S
National Aquarium, Baltimore, Maryland	$4.00	$3.00	$2.00	S
National Capitol, Waters Souvenir Co., 1900			$80.00	S
National Cowboy Hall of Fame, Oklahoma	$4.00	$3.00	$2.00	S
National Life Insurance	$4.00	$3.00	$2.00	S
National Safety Council, Green Cross for Safety	$8.00	$6.00	$4.00	S
Nations Capitol, Standing Liberty, USPC, 1 Joker, 1922	$125.00	$75.00	$50.00	S
Native Americans, U.S. Games, 1996	$6.00	$4.50	$3.00	S
Naval Warship Spotters, 1940s–1960s Ships, 1970s Issue	$16.00	$12.00	$8.00	S
NCL, First Fleet of the Caribbean, Cruise Ship	$4.00	$3.00	$2.00	S
Nebraska Cornhuskers, University	$5.00	$4.00	$2.50	S
Neiman Marcus Department Store	$10.00	$7.50	$5.00	S
Nevada Club, Casino	$2.00	$1.50	$1.00	S
New England Mutual Life Insurance Company, Clock Tower	$4.00	$3.00	$2.00	S
New England Patriots	$6.00	$4.50	$3.00	S
New Hampshire, Moose, Tourist, Plastic Case	$4.00	$3.00	$2.00	S
New Jersey Devils	$6.00	$4.50	$3.00	S
New Jersey Nets	$6.00	$4.50	$3.00	S
New Orleans Hornets	$4.00	$3.00	$2.00	S
New Orleans Saints	$6.00	$4.50	$3.00	S
New Orleans World Fair, 1984	$6.00	$4.50	$3.00	S
The New York Central System, Railroad	$8.00	$6.00	$4.00	S
New York City, Early 20th Century Tourist Deck		$75.00	$50.00	S
New York Consolidated Card Co., DD 1930s Set in Slipcase		$20.00	$12.50	DD
New York Giants	$6.00	$4.50	$3.00	S
New York Islanders	$6.00	$4.50	$3.00	S
New York Jets	$6.00	$4.50	$3.00	S
New York Knicks	$6.00	$4.50	$3.00	S
New York Mets	$6.00	$4.50	$3.00	S
The New York, New Haven, and Hartford Railroad Co.	$4.00	$3.00	$2.00	S
New York New York, Casino	$2.00	$1.50	$1.00	S
New York Rangers	$6.00	$4.50	$3.00	S
New York World's Fair, Double Deck Set, 1939	$125.00	$100.00	$75.00	DD
New York World's Fair, DD Set, Stancraft, 1964-1965, Plastic Case	$12.00	$9.00	$6.00	S
New York Yankees	$6.00	$4.50	$3.00	S
Newport Cigarettes	$6.00	$4.50	$3.00	S
NFL, Double Deck Set in Tin (Decorated w. Field), 1990s	$10.00	$7.50	$5.00	DD
NFL Football Stars, Players on all Cards, 1992	$6.00	$4.50	$3.00	S
NHL Heritage Collection, Jerseys & Stadiums, 1990s	$6.00	$4.50	$3.00	S
NHL Eastern Conference Stars, Players on all Cards, 1992	$6.00	$4.50	$3.00	S
NHL Western Conference Stars, Players on all Cards, 1992	$6.00	$4.50	$3.00	S
Niagara Falls, Tourist	$4.00	$3.00	$2.00	S
Niagara Falls, Tourist, Mini Deck, Plastic Case	$3.00	$2.00	$1.50	M
Nickel Plate Road, Railroad	$8.00	$6.00	$4.00	S
Nightmare Before Christmas Movie Deck	$8.00	$6.00	$4.00	S
Nikolai Vodka	$8.00	$6.00	$4.00	S
Nile Fortune Cards, Copyright 1897–1904	$125.00	$75.00	$50.00	S
Nor by Northbrook Brand, 1950s	$3.00	$2.00	$1.50	S
Norfolk Southern, Railroad	$8.00	$6.00	$4.00	S

Norman Rockwell, Painting, Fall	$6.00	$4.50	$3.00	S
Norman Rockwell, Painting, Spring	$6.00	$4.50	$3.00	S
Norman Rockwell, Painting, Summer	$6.00	$4.50	$3.00	S
Norman Rockwell, Painting, Winter	$6.00	$4.50	$3.00	S
Norman Rockwell Paintings, Double Deck Set	$12.00	$9.00	$6.00	DD
Norman Rockwell Paintings, Double Deck Set in Tin	$16.00	$12.00	$8.00	DD
North American Van Lines	$4.00	$3.00	$2.00	S
North American Van Lines, Moving Van	$6.00	$4.50	$3.00	S
North Carolina Tarheels, University	$5.00	$4.00	$2.50	S
North Carolina State University Wolves	$5.00	$4.00	$2.50	S
North Dakota, Bed & Breakfast Frames, Souvenir	$4.00	$3.00	$2.00	S
North Dakota State Outline	$1.00	$0.75	$0.50	S
Northeastern, NE 880 Jets	$5.00	$4.00	$2.50	S
Northern Pacific Railway	$8.00	$6.00	$4.00	S
Northern Quest Casino	$2.00	$1.50	$1.00	S
Northwest Airlines, Jet	$6.00	$4.50	$3.00	S
Northwest Airlines, Lettering Only	$4.00	$3.00	$2.00	S
Northwest Paper Company, Horse & Mountie	$6.00	$4.50	$3.00	S
Northwestern Wildcats, University	$5.00	$4.00	$2.50	S
Norwalk 5 Ply Tire, Large Tire	$4.00	$3.00	$2.00	S
Norway, Norwegian Caribbean Lines, Cruise Ship	$6.00	$4.50	$3.00	S
Norway, Norwegian Caribbean Lines, Lettering Only	$4.00	$3.00	$2.00	S
Norwegian Lines, Cruise Ship	$6.00	$4.50	$3.00	S
Notre Dame Fighting Irish, University	$5.00	$4.00	$2.50	S
Notre Dame, University, 1950s	$6.00	$4.50	$3.00	S
No.88 Deer Club Special Brand	$1.50	$1.00	$0.75	S
No.88 Deer Club Special Brand, Buck Backs	$2.00	$1.50	$1.00	S
Oakland A's or Athletics	$6.00	$4.50	$3.00	S
Oakland Raiders	$6.00	$4.50	$3.00	S
Ocean's 11, Movie, Single Deck in Tin	$8.00	$6.00	$4.00	S
O'Doul's Premium Nonalcoholic Brew	$6.00	$4.50	$3.00	S
Ohio State Buckeyes, University	$5.00	$4.00	$2.50	S
Oklahoma Sooners	$5.00	$4.00	$2.50	S
Oklahoma State University	$5.00	$4.00	$2.50	S
Old Bushmills Black Bush Irish Blended Whiskey	$10.00	$7.50	$5.00	S
Old Curiosity Shop, English, Double Deck Set	$16.00	$12.00	$8.00	DD
Old Farmers Insurance Group, Building	$4.00	$3.00	$2.00	S
Old Geezer, Novelty Deck on Aging	$4.00	$3.00	$2.00	S
Old Gold Cigarettes	$6.00	$4.50	$3.00	S
Old Gold Lights, Cigarettes	$6.00	$4.50	$3.00	S
Old Holdborn Red Rum	$10.00	$7.50	$5.00	S
Old Huckleberry Bourbon	$10.00	$7.50	$5.00	S
Old Milwaukee Genuine Draft Beer, Tastes as Great as its Name	$6.00	$4.50	$3.00	S
Old Navy, Department Store, Egg-Shaped Deck in Plastic Case	$6.00	$4.50	$3.00	U
Old Style Beer, Bavarian Couple	$6.00	$4.50	$3.00	S
Old Style Beer, Can-Shaped	$10.00	$7.50	$5.00	S
Old Style Beer, Man with Bottle & Glass	$6.00	$4.50	$3.00	S
Old Style Beer, Men Drinking at Table	$6.00	$4.50	$3.00	S
Old Train, Ace World Famous Arts	$8.00	$6.00	$4.00	S
Ole Miss Rebels, University	$5.00	$4.00	$2.50	S
Olds is 3rd!, Two Oldsmobile Cars	$6.00	$4.50	$3.00	S
Olympia Beer, 2-Deck Portrait Ladies' Set in Olympia Box	$12.00	$9.00	$6.00	DD
Omaha Brand	$2.00	$1.50	$1.00	S
100 Pipers Scotch by Seagram	$6.00	$4.50	$3.00	S
101 Dalmatians, Double Deck Set, 1980s	$10.00	$7.50	$5.00	DD
Opryland, Tennessee	$4.00	$3.00	$2.00	S
Oral B Toothbrush	$8.00	$6.00	$4.00	S
Oregon Ducks, University	$5.00	$4.00	$2.50	S
Oregon Pacific & Eastern Railway	$6.00	$4.50	$3.00	S
Oregon State University Beavers	$5.00	$4.00	$2.50	S
Orlando Magic	$6.00	$4.50	$3.00	S
Ostend Dover, Cruise Lines	$6.00	$4.50	$3.00	S
Ottawa Senators	$6.00	$4.50	$3.00	S
Overland Hotel & Casino	$2.00	$1.50	$1.00	S
Overseas National Airways, Jet in Globe	$5.00	$4.00	$2.50	S
Ozark Airlines	$5.00	$4.00	$2.50	S
Ozark Flies Your Way, Colorado, White Water Rafting	$8.00	$6.00	$4.00	S
Ozark Flies Your Way, New York, Statue of Liberty	$8.00	$6.00	$4.00	S
Ozark Flies Your Way, 1984 World's Fair New Orleans	$8.00	$6.00	$4.00	S
Ozark Flies Your Way, San Diego, Sailboat	$8.00	$6.00	$4.00	S
P & O, Bamboo in Oval	$5.00	$4.00	$2.50	DD
P & O, Suit Symbols in Concentric Circles	$5.00	$4.00	$2.50	S
P & Orient, Oriental Face Card	$5.00	$4.00	$2.50	S
Pabst Blue Ribbon Beer, Can Design, 1950s	$15.00	$10.00	$7.50	S
Pacific Electric, Comfort Speed Safety, Railroad	$4.00	$3.00	$2.00	S
Pacific Far East Line, Bear in Circle, SS Mariposa, SS Monterey	$6.00	$4.50	$3.00	S
Pacific Northwest	$3.00	$2.00	$1.50	S
Pacific Western Airlines, Jet, We're With You All The Way	$5.00	$4.00	$2.50	S
Paddy Old Irish Whiskey	$10.00	$7.50	$5.00	S
Painted Desert, Arizona, Tourist	$4.00	$3.00	$2.00	S
Palace Club Casino	$2.00	$1.50	$1.00	S
Palace Station Casino	$2.00	$1.50	$1.00	S
Pall Mall Cigarettes, Various Pack Designs	$6.00	$4.50	$3.00	S
Pan Am, Elephant by River	$8.00	$6.00	$4.00	S
Pan Am, Reflecting Trees in River Scene	$5.00	$4.00	$2.50	S
Pan American, Globe, World's Most Experienced Airline	$5.00	$4.00	$2.50	S
Pan American, Large Jet	$8.00	$6.00	$4.00	S
Pan American World Airways, Winged Globe	$8.00	$6.00	$4.00	S
Panama Inaugural, 1915			$75.00	S
Panama Canal, Steamship, USPC, 1923		$80.00	$60.00	S
Panasonic Car Stereo and Speakers, Speaker	$4.00	$3.00	$2.00	S
Paris Hotel & Casino	$2.00	$1.50	$1.00	S
Paris Story, Philibert	$40.00	$30.00	$20.00	S

Paris, Framed City Scenes, Tourist, Plastic Case	$5.00	$4.00	$2.50	S
Park Drive Cigarettes, 1940s	$20.00	$15.00	$10.00	S
Parthenon, Nashville, Tennessee	$2.00	$1.50	$1.00	S
Patriotic Tribute, American Soldier	$5.00	$4.00	$2.50	S
Paulson, Brand	$2.00	$1.50	$1.00	S
Paulson, Casino	$2.00	$1.50	$1.00	S
Paulson Gaming Supplies	$2.00	$1.50	$1.00	S
Peacock Brand, France, Peacock Style Aces	$8.00	$6.00	$4.00	S
Peanuts, Comic Characters on All Cards, Various Designs	$8.00	$6.00	$4.00	S
Pearl Beer	$8.00	$6.00	$4.00	S
Pearl Light Beer	$8.00	$6.00	$4.00	S
Pella Windows, Doors, Rolscreens	$4.00	$3.00	$2.00	S
Penn Central, Railroad	$6.00	$4.50	$3.00	S
Penn Mutual, Insurance, Buildings in Circle	$4.00	$3.00	$2.00	S
Penn State University Nittany Lions	$5.00	$4.00	$2.50	S
Pennsylvania Railroad, Symbol Only	$8.00	$6.00	$4.00	S
Pennsylvania Railroad, 48-Card Pinochle Deck	$10.00	$7.50	$5.00	S
Pennsylvania, State Outline, Tourist, Plastic Case	$4.00	$3.00	$2.00	S
Peoples Brand	$2.00	$1.50	$1.00	S
Pepperidge Farms, Mixed Suits, 1960s	$8.00	$6.00	$4.00	S
Pepsi Cola, Many Designs	$6.00	$4.50	$3.00	S
Pete's Wicked Winter Brew	$10.00	$7.50	$5.00	S
Peter Dawson Scotch	$10.00	$7.50	$5.00	S
Peter Pan Miniature Playing Cards	$6.00	$4.50	$3.00	M
Petty, Pin-Up Girl with Bugle, 1 Joker, 1960		$30.00	$20.00	S
Philadelphia Eagles	$6.00	$4.50	$3.00	S
Philadelphia Flyers	$6.00	$4.50	$3.00	S
Philadelphia Phillies	$6.00	$4.50	$3.00	S
Philadelphia 76ers	$6.00	$4.50	$3.00	S
Phillip Morris 100s Cigarettes	$6.00	$4.50	$3.00	S
Phillip Morris, Star Deck in Tin with Poker Dice	$8.00	$6.00	$4.00	S
Phillips 66, Gas Logo	$6.00	$4.50	$3.00	S
Piccadilly Circus, London	$3.00	$2.00	$1.50	S
Phoenix Cardinals	$6.00	$4.50	$3.00	S
Phoenix Coffee, 1950s	$8.00	$6.00	$4.00	S
Phoenix Coyotes	$6.00	$4.50	$3.00	S
Phoenix Suns	$6.00	$4.50	$3.00	S
Piatnik of Austria, Double Mini Deck, Gold Edged, Bird Backs, 1950s	$40.00	$30.00	$20.00	DD/M
Piatnik of Austria, Double Tiny Deck, 1 3/4" x 1 1/8", 1950s	$40.00	$30.00	$20.00	DD/T
Piedmont Airlines, Various	$5.00	$4.00	$2.50	S
Pike National Forest	$4.00	$3.00	$2.00	S
Pike's Peak, Colorado	$4.00	$3.00	$2.00	S
Pillsbury Plus Cake Mix	$10.00	$7.50	$5.00	S
Pink Floyd Dark Side of the Moon	$8.00	$6.00	$4.00	S
Pinocchio, Disney Film Version, 1950s	$12.00	$9.00	$6.00	S
Pin-Up Girls, Modern, 1970s–Up (aka Adult, Gaiety, Nude Models)	$5.00	$4.00	$2.50	S
Pin-Up Girls, Older, 1950s–1960s	$12.00	$9.00	$6.00	S
Pin-Up Girls, Antique, 1940s & Before	$20.00	$15.00	$10.00	S
Pin-Up Models, Asian, 1960s, Mini Deck	$12.00	$9.00	$6.00	M
Piper-Heidsieck Champagne	$6.00	$4.50	$3.00	S
Pirates of the Caribbean, Movie Deck	$6.00	$4.50	$3.00	S
Pirates Playing Cards	$4.00	$3.00	$2.00	S
Pirate Poker	$4.00	$3.00	$2.00	S
Pisa, Leaning Tower, Italy, Tourist	$5.00	$4.00	$2.50	S
Pisces the Fishes, Zodiac Sign, 1960s	$10.00	$7.50	$5.00	S
Pittsburgh Penguins	$6.00	$4.50	$3.00	S
Pittsburgh Pirates	$6.00	$4.50	$3.00	S
Pittsburgh Steelers	$6.00	$4.50	$3.00	S
Pizza Hut, Double Deck Set	$12.00	$9.00	$6.00	S
Planters Peanuts, Peanut Boat, 1930s	$125.00	$75.00	$50.00	S
Playboy Bunny, White Bunny Head Logo	$10.00	$7.50	$5.00	S
Playboy Playmate, 1973, Double Set	$20.00	$15.00	$10.00	DD
Plaza Hotel & Casino	$2.00	$1.50	$1.00	S
Plymouth, Massachusetts, Mini Deck, Plastic Case	$3.00	$2.00	$1.50	M
Pokemon, 3-Deck Set Playing Cards in Plastic Case, Half-Size Cards	$20.00	$15.00	$10.00	U
Politicards, Caricature Face Cards, Politicard Co., 1971	$20.00	$15.00	$10.00	S
Polish Playing Cards	$6.00	$4.50	$3.00	S
Politicards, 1996	$6.00	$4.50	$3.00	S
Pooh & Friends, Disney Mini Deck	$4.00	$3.00	$2.00	M
Porky & Petunia Pig, Looney Tunes, 1990s	$8.00	$6.00	$4.00	S
Portland Trail Blazers	$6.00	$4.50	$3.00	S
Power Rangers, Mystic Force Die Cut	$4.00	$3.00	$2.00	S
Power Rangers, Television Show, 1990s	$6.00	$4.50	$3.00	S
Power's Blended Irish Whiskey	$10.00	$7.50	$5.00	S
Presidents of the U.S., Washington through Bush Sr., 1990 Issue	$6.00	$4.50	$3.00	S
Primadonna, Casino	$2.00	$1.50	$1.00	S
Primo Hawaiian Beer	$10.00	$7.50	$5.00	S
Prince Charles & Diana, Double Deck Wedding Set, July 29, 1981	$40.00	$35.00	$30.00	DD
Princess Cruises	$5.00	$4.00	$2.50	S
Pro Football Hall of Fame, Canton, Ohio	$4.00	$3.00	$2.00	S
Proctor & Gamble	$6.00	$4.50	$3.00	S
Providence & Worcester Railroad	$6.00	$4.50	$3.00	S
Prudential Lines, Insurance	$4.00	$3.00	$2.00	S
Pullman Railway Car, 1915			$75.00	S
Pullman Railway Car, Special Aces, 1942			$25.00	S
Pullman, Travel and Sleep in Comfort and Safety	$6.00	$4.50	$3.00	S
Purdue Boilermakers, University	$5.00	$4.00	$2.50	S
Qantas Airlines	$6.00	$4.50	$3.00	S
Qantas Airlines, Round Deck	$10.00	$7.50	$5.00	R
Quebec Nordiques	$6.00	$4.50	$3.00	S
Queen High Quality, Emjay Co., Women's Liberation, 1971	$30.00	$25.00	$20.00	S
Queen Elizabeth Silver Jubilee, Portraits	$12.00	$9.00	$6.00	S
Queen Mary II, Large Cruise Ship	$10.00	$7.50	$5.00	S
Queen Victoria Golden Jubilee, 1887			$125.00	S
Quest Software	$2.00	$1.50	$1.00	S
Quickrete, Yellow Concrete Bag	$6.00	$4.50	$3.00	S

Rahr, Malt of Reputation	$8.00	$6.00	$4.00	S
Raid Kills Bugs Dead	$4.00	$3.00	$2.00	S
Railroads, Multiple Logos	$6.00	$4.50	$3.00	S
Rainbow Trout, State-O-Maine Brand	$10.00	$7.50	$5.00	S
Rainforest Café	$8.00	$6.00	$4.00	S
Raleigh Cigarettes	$6.00	$4.50	$3.00	S
Rally Brand	$2.00	$1.50	$1.00	S
Rayovac Batteries	$6.00	$4.50	$3.00	S
RC Cola	$6.00	$4.50	$3.00	S
RCA	$4.00	$3.00	$2.00	S
RCA ColorTrak	$4.00	$3.00	$2.00	S
Reading Lines, Railroad	$12.00	$9.00	$6.00	S
Realtree Hardwoods	$2.00	$1.50	$1.00	S
Rebel or Confederate Flag	$4.00	$3.00	$2.00	S
Red Dog Beer, Large Bulldog Head	$10.00	$7.50	$5.00	S
Red Hat Society	$6.00	$4.50	$3.00	S
Red N Blue Brand	$2.00	$1.50	$1.00	S
Red Star Line, Santa Maria Backs, 1942			$50.00	S
Reddington Electric Service Co., Boston, c.1912			$30.00	S
Reddy Kilowatt, 48-Card Pinochle Deck	$20.00	$15.00	$10.00	S
Reddy Kilowatt, USPC, Face on Power Plug	$40.00	$30.00	$20.00	S
Redislip Brand	$2.00	$1.50	$1.00	S
Regal Cigarettes	$6.00	$4.50	$3.00	S
Remembrance Brand, Brown & Bigelow, Gold Foil Box, 1960s	$5.00	$4.00	$2.50	S
Remembrance Brand, Brown & Bigelow, Redi-Slip	$1.00	$0.75	$0.50	S
Remington, First in the Field, Ducks	$6.00	$4.50	$3.00	S
Reno, Nevada, Tourist Deck	$3.00	$2.00	$1.50	S
Republic Airlines	$4.00	$3.00	$2.00	S
REVCO, Company Logo	$4.00	$3.00	$2.00	S
Rexall Brand	$1.50	$1.00	$0.50	S
Rhode Island, State Photos in each Card, 1 Joker, USPC, 1910		$100.00	$75.00	S
Richmond Fredericksburg and Potomac Railroad Co.	$4.00	$3.00	$2.00	S
Richmond Washington Line, Railroad	$4.00	$3.00	$2.00	S
Rio Grande, The Action Railroad	$6.00	$4.50	$3.00	S
Rio Grande, Main Line, Through the Rockies, Mountain Scene	$16.00	$12.00	$8.00	S
Rite Aid Drug Stores	$3.00	$2.00	$1.50	S
River Palms, Casino	$2.00	$1.50	$1.00	S
Riviera Casino	$2.00	$1.50	$1.00	S
Riviera Slot World	$3.00	$2.00	$1.50	S
Robert E. Lee Riverboat, Double Deck set in Tin	$16.00	$12.00	$8.00	DD
Robo, Car & Carwash, 1960s	$8.00	$6.00	$4.00	S
Robo, Wax Job, Carwash, 1960s	$8.00	$6.00	$4.00	S
Rock & Roll Hall of Fame, Cleveland, Ohio	$5.00	$4.00	$2.50	S
Rock City, Lookout Mountain, Tennessee or Georgia	$4.00	$3.00	$2.00	S
Rock Island, Railroad	$8.00	$6.00	$4.00	S
Rock Island Route, Railroad, Early 1900s Deck in Case	$100.00	$75.00	$50.00	S
Rockwell International, Face Cards with Astronaut Suits, 1980	$25.00	$17.50	$12.50	S
Rockwell International, Missile Systems Division	$6.00	$4.50	$3.00	S
Rockwell Standard	$4.00	$3.00	$2.00	S
Rocky Mountains Concessions, Man on Mule, 1889			$75.00	S
Rococo, Piatnik, Double Deck Set	$12.00	$9.00	$6.00	DD
Rodeo	$2.00	$1.50	$1.00	S
Rolling Stones, Tongue Logo	$12.00	$9.00	$6.00	S
Rolls Royce, Gold Edges, Universal, 1960	$15.00	$10.00	$7.50	S
Rolls Royce, Gold Luxury Automobile	$20.00	$15.00	$10.00	S
Romanov, Piatnik, Double Deck Set	$12.00	$9.00	$6.00	DD
Rose-Hulman Institute of Technology	$4.00	$3.00	$2.00	S
Round Decks	$5.00	$4.00	$2.50	R
Round Deck, I.N. Richardson, 5 King Heads on Back, 1874			$150.00	R
Route 66	$5.00	$4.00	$2.50	S
Royal Brand, French, Les Jeux Des Cartes	$1.50	$1.00	$0.50	S
Royal Brand, New York	$2.00	$1.50	$1.00	S
Royal Caribbean Cruise Line, Ship, Repeated on Opposite Side	$6.00	$4.50	$3.00	S
Royal Cruise Line, Aspiota Elka Ltd.	$6.00	$4.50	$3.00	S
Royal Gorge Route Scenic Line, Railroad	$8.00	$6.00	$4.00	S
Rubberset Shaving & Tooth Brush Advertising, 1920		$35.00	$25.00	S
Ruby Falls, Tin Box	$4.00	$3.00	$2.00	S
Ruilong Brand	$2.00	$1.50	$1.00	S
Rust-Oleum, Sailing Ship	$8.00	$6.00	$4.00	S
Ruxton Brand	$2.00	$1.50	$1.00	S
Ruxton Brand—1940s & Earlier	$12.00	$9.00	$6.00	S
Ryder Truck Rental	$6.00	$4.50	$3.00	S
Sabena, Small Jets & Helicopters, Belgian World Airlines	$5.00	$4.00	$2.50	S
Sacramento Kings	$6.00	$4.50	$3.00	S
Sacramento Northern, Through the Sacramento Valley, Railroad	$6.00	$4.50	$3.00	S
SAE, Society of Automotive Engineers, Double Deck Set	$4.00	$3.00	$2.00	DD
Sagittarius the Archer, Zodiac Sign, 1960s	$10.00	$7.50	$5.00	S
Sahara Hotel & Casino	$2.00	$1.50	$1.00	S
Sahara Tahoe, Casino	$2.00	$1.50	$1.00	S
Sailboats, Rhode Island, Tourist	$4.00	$3.00	$2.00	S
St. Joseph, Missouri, 1907 Landmark Deck	$500.00	$150.00	$100.00	S
St. Louis Arch, St. Louis, Missouri, Tourist	$4.00	$3.00	$2.00	S
St. Louis Blues	$6.00	$4.50	$3.00	S
St. Louis Cardinals	$6.00	$4.50	$3.00	S
St. Louis Rams	$6.00	$4.50	$3.00	S
St. Louis Tourist, Framed Designs, Single Deck in Decorated Tin	$6.00	$4.50	$3.00	S
Saks 34th St., Special Aces, 1920s			$75.00	S
Salem Cigarettes, Various Designs	$6.00	$4.50	$3.00	S
Salem Witch Museum; Witch, Broom, & Black Cat Design	$8.00	$6.00	$4.00	S
Samba, American Three Deck Canasta Set (triple deck)	$4.00	$3.00	$2.00	TD
San Antonio Spurs	$6.00	$4.50	$3.00	S
San Diego Chargers	$6.00	$4.50	$3.00	S
San Diego Padres	$6.00	$4.50	$3.00	S
San Jose Sharks	$6.00	$4.50	$3.00	S
San Diego State University	$4.00	$3.00	$2.00	S
San Francisco 49ers	$6.00	$4.50	$3.00	S
San Francisco Giants	$6.00	$4.50	$3.00	S
Sands, Casino	$2.00	$1.50	$1.00	S

Santa Clara University	$4.00	$3.00	$2.00	S
Santa Clausland, Indiana	$3.00	$2.00	$1.50	S
Santa Fe, Casino	$2.00	$1.50	$1.00	S
Santa Fe, 1818 Engine	$10.00	$7.50	$5.00	S
Santa Fe, 5695 Engine	$10.00	$7.50	$5.00	S
Santa Fe, 5695 & 5696 Engines, Double Set	$20.00	$15.00	$10.00	DD
Santa Fe, Railroad, General	$10.00	$7.50	$5.00	S
Santa Fe, Two Trains, Desert Scenery, Bridge, Several Styles	$30.00	$22.50	$15.00	S
SAS Airline	$5.00	$4.00	$2.50	S
Saturday Evening Post, Norman Rockwell, Double Deck Set in Tin	$12.00	$9.00	$6.00	DD
Savings of America	$1.00	$0.75	$0.50	S
Scarface, Movie Deck	$10.00	$7.50	$5.00	S
Schaefer, America's Oldest Lager Beer	$4.00	$3.00	$2.00	S
Schlitz Beer, Globe	$8.00	$6.00	$4.00	S
Schlitz, The Beer that made Milwaukee Famous	$8.00	$6.00	$4.00	S
Schlitz Malt Liquor, Bull	$8.00	$6.00	$4.00	S
Scooby-Doo, Cartoon Network	$4.00	$3.00	$2.00	S
Scooby-Doo Mini Deck	$3.00	$2.00	$1.50	M
Scoresby Scotch Whiskey	$10.00	$7.50	$5.00	S
Scorpio the Scorpion, Zodiac Sign, 1960s	$10.00	$7.50	$5.00	S
Scripps Institution of Oceanography	$4.00	$3.00	$2.00	S
Sea Shells	$1.00	$0.75	$0.50	S
Sea World, Various Tourist Decks	$4.00	$3.00	$2.00	S
Seaboard & Western Airlines, Jet	$8.00	$6.00	$4.00	S
Seaboard Coast Line Railroad	$6.00	$4.50	$3.00	S
Seaboard Railroad, Through the Heart of the South	$8.00	$6.00	$4.00	S
Seaboard System Railroad	$6.00	$4.50	$3.00	S
Seagrams Gin	$8.00	$6.00	$4.00	S
Seagrams Whiskey	$8.00	$6.00	$4.00	S
Sealtest Ice Cream & Milk	$4.00	$3.00	$2.00	S
Sears Tower, Chicago, Illinois	$4.00	$3.00	$2.00	S
Seashore Trolley Museum, Kennebunkport, Maine	$4.00	$3.00	$2.00	S
Seattle Mariners	$6.00	$4.50	$3.00	S
Seattle Seahawks	$6.00	$4.50	$3.00	S
Seattle Supersonics	$6.00	$4.50	$3.00	S
Seattle Tourist Deck in Tin	$4.00	$3.00	$2.00	S
Second Empire, French Transformation Deck, 1860, Hand-Tinted			$2,500	U
See-Thru Deck	$4.00	$3.00	$2.00	S
Servel Refrigerators, 1950s, Double Deck Set	$6.00	$4.50	$3.00	DD
7-UP, Soft Drink Logo, Various Designs	$8.00	$6.00	$4.00	S
7-UP, The Spot, Special 7-UP Card Inside	$10.00	$7.50	$5.00	S
Shakespeare, Piatnik, Double Deck Set, 1980s	$12.00	$9.00	$6.00	DD
The Shamrock, Hotel, Houston	$4.00	$3.00	$2.00	S
Shamrock, Piatnik, Double Deck Set	$12.00	$9.00	$6.00	DD
Shell Gas Logo	$8.00	$6.00	$4.00	S
Shell Super X Motor Oil, Can Design, 1950s	$12.00	$9.00	$6.00	S
Shepherd of the Hills Farm	$4.00	$3.00	$2.00	S
Sherwin Williams	$6.00	$4.50	$3.00	S
Shiloh National Military Park, Shiloh, Tennessee	$5.00	$4.00	$2.50	S
Shoebox Greetings by Hallmark, Double Deck Set, Piatnik	$8.00	$6.00	$4.00	DD
Show Girls, Scantily Clad or Naked	$5.00	$4.00	$2.50	S
Show World Air Express, United Van Lines	$4.00	$3.00	$2.00	S
Shrek II, Animated Film, Double Deck Set in Tin	$12.00	$9.00	$6.00	DD
Sierra Railroad Company, Rail Transportation	$4.00	$3.00	$2.00	S
Sigillum College Gettysburg, Pennsylvania	$4.00	$3.00	$2.00	S
Silver Art Deck, Latched Plastic Case, Unique Card Designs	$8.00	$6.00	$4.00	S
Silver City, Casino	$2.00	$1.50	$1.00	S
Silver Club, Casino	$2.00	$1.50	$1.00	S
Silver Nugget, Casino	$2.00	$1.50	$1.00	S
Silver Slipper, Casino	$2.00	$1.50	$1.00	S
The Simpsons, Cartoon, Bart Simpson Round Deck	$4.00	$3.00	$2.00	R
The Simpsons, Cartoon, Bart Simpson with Slingshot, in Tin	$6.00	$4.50	$3.00	S
The Simpsons, Cartoon, Homer Simpson Round Deck	$4.00	$3.00	$2.00	R
The Simpsons, Cartoon, Deck in 12 oz. Duff Beer Tin Can Bank	$20.00	$15.00	$10.00	U
Sinclair Gas, Dinosaur Logo	$10.00	$7.50	$5.00	S
Sinclair Oils, Oil Well in Circle	$4.00	$3.00	$2.00	S
Sitting Bull Indian Chief at Capitol Bldg., Congress, USPC, 1890s			$300.00	S
Six Flags, Texas	$4.00	$3.00	$2.00	S
Skagway, Alaska, Train on Tin & Card Backs, 1 Deck in Tin	$12.00	$9.00	$6.00	S
SKAL, Airliner, Jet	$6.00	$4.50	$3.00	S
Skoal, Bandit Tobacco	$4.00	$3.00	$2.00	S
Slot World, Casino	$2.00	$1.50	$1.00	S
Slots A Fun, Casino	$2.00	$1.50	$1.00	S
Small Soldiers, Animated Film	$8.00	$6.00	$4.00	S
Smiley Face, Large Yellow Face	$5.00	$4.00	$2.50	S
Smirnoff Brands, VAT 69, Cinzano, Piper-Heidsieck, etc.	$6.00	$4.50	$3.00	S
Smirnoff Vodka, Bottle	$6.00	$4.50	$3.00	S
Smirnoff Vodka, Special Company Logo Jokers	$10.00	$7.50	$5.00	S
Smithsonian	$4.00	$3.00	$2.00	S
S'Mores Original	$5.00	$4.00	$2.50	S
Snap-On Tools	$8.00	$6.00	$4.00	S
Snatch, Movie Deck	$8.00	$6.00	$4.00	S
Snirkles, A Really Good Caramel Bar	$4.00	$3.00	$2.00	S
Snoopy, Peanuts Character, Various Back Designs	$8.00	$6.00	$4.00	S
Snow White & the 7 Dwarfs, Disney, 1950s	$12.00	$9.00	$6.00	S
Soaring Eagle, Casino	$2.00	$1.50	$1.00	S
Sobelair, Jets & Pips	$5.00	$4.00	$2.50	S
Society Series, Slipcase, 1890s– Early 1900s, Various Designs		$75.00	$50.00	S
SOHIO, Gas Logo	$6.00	$4.50	$3.00	S
SOHIO, Gas Logo, Eagle	$8.00	$6.00	$4.00	S
Soo Line, Railroad, Logo/ Lettering Only	$4.00	$3.00	$2.00	S
Soo Line, Railroad, Rural Scene	$30.00	$22.50	$15.00	S
Soo The Milwaukee Road, Railroad	$8.00	$6.00	$4.00	S
The Sopranos, HBO Television Series	$16.00	$12.00	$8.00	S
South Dakota, Badlands, Blackhills, Mt. Rushmore, Various	$2.00	$1.50	$1.00	S
South Park, Cartoon, Single Deck in Tin	$10.00	$7.50	$5.00	S
Southern Airways, Jet	$6.00	$4.50	$3.00	S
Southern Airways, Lettering Only	$4.00	$3.00	$2.00	S

Southern Comfort Bourbon, Rural Southern Plantation Scene	$10.00	$7.50	$5.00	S
Southern Pacific Lines, Railroad	$8.00	$6.00	$4.00	S
Southern Pacific Railroad, 1910, Blue Case	$80.00	$60.00	$40.00	S
The Southern Serves the South, Railroad	$8.00	$6.00	$4.00	S
Southwest Airlines	$4.00	$3.00	$2.00	S
Southwest Airlines, Coca-Cola Promotion, 2004	$4.00	$3.00	$2.00	S
Souvenir Brand	$2.00	$1.50	$1.00	S
Space Center, Huntsville, Alabama	$4.00	$3.00	$2.00	S
Space Needle, Seattle, Washington	$4.00	$3.00	$2.00	S
Space Shuttle, Kennedy Space Center, Florida	$5.00	$4.00	$2.50	S
Spider-Man, Marvel Comics	$8.00	$6.00	$4.00	S
Spider-Man, Motion Picture	$8.00	$6.00	$4.00	S
Spider-Man 3, Movie, 4 Deck Mini Set	$12.00	$9.00	$6.00	M
Spokane Portland and Seattle Ry., Railroad	$4.00	$3.00	$2.00	S
Sponge Bob, Cartoon Characters	$8.00	$6.00	$4.00	S
Sponge Bob Mini Deck	$4.00	$3.00	$2.00	M
Sponge Bob Nickelodeon	$8.00	$6.00	$4.00	S
Sponge Bob Nickelodeon Double Deck Set in Tin	$16.00	$12.00	$8.00	DD
Sportsman Series	$4.00	$3.00	$2.00	S
Spotters, 1984 U.S. Army Armored Vehicles	$12.00	$9.00	$6.00	S
Spotters, 2005 WWII Replica Deck	$4.00	$3.00	$2.00	S
Squires London Dry Gin	$6.00	$4.50	$3.00	S
Stag Beer, Carling, Can-Shape	$10.00	$7.50	$5.00	S
Stag Party Pack	$12.00	$9.00	$6.00	S
Stage #65X, Cameo Girl, 1 Joker, USPC, 1908			$125.00	S
Stancraft Stop Watches, Gold Pocket Watches, 2-Deck Set, 1960	$16.00	$12.00	$8.00	DD
Standard Oil	$6.00	$4.50	$3.00	S
Standard Oil Company, 1932	$50.00	$40.00	$30.00	S
Star Trek, Single Deck, 1960s	$16.00	$12.00	$8.00	S
Star Trek, Double Deck Set in Tin, Original Series, 1990s	$16.00	$12.00	$8.00	DD
Star Trek Next Generation, Double Deck Set in Tin	$12.00	$9.00	$6.00	DD
Star Wars, Episode I, Movie, Asian Deck	$8.00	$6.00	$4.00	S
Star Wars, Episode I, Movie, Canadian Deck	$12.00	$9.00	$6.00	S
Star Wars, Heroes & Villains	$10.00	$7.50	$5.00	S
Star Wars, Vehicles	$10.00	$7.50	$5.00	S
Stardust Hotel, Casino	$2.00	$1.50	$1.00	S
Starz Behind Barz, Celebrity Mug Shots	$4.00	$3.00	$2.00	S
State Farm Insurance Company, Company Logo	$4.00	$3.00	$2.00	S
States Marine Lines, Flag in Life Float Logo, Various Styles	$6.00	$4.50	$3.00	S
Statue of Liberty, New York	$5.00	$4.00	$2.50	S
Steamboat, Colorado, Tourist	$4.00	$3.00	$2.00	S
Steamboat, New Mexico, Tourist	$4.00	$3.00	$2.00	S
Steamboat, #999 Brand with Steamboat Jokers, 1955	$12.00	$9.00	$6.00	S
Stock Index	$3.00	$2.00	$1.50	S
Stone Mountain, Georgia	$4.00	$3.00	$2.00	S
Strasburg Railroad	$6.00	$4.50	$3.00	S
Stratosphere Hotel & Casino	$2.00	$1.50	$1.00	S
Stratus Brand	$2.00	$1.50	$1.00	S
Streamline No. 1 Brand	$2.00	$1.50	$1.00	S
Streamline Pinochle, U.S. Gov't Issue, Linen Finish, 48 Cards, 1940s	$6.00	$4.50	$3.00	P
Stroh's Beer For Beer Lovers, Logo	$8.00	$6.00	$4.00	S
Stud Brand, Stallion Backs	$2.00	$1.50	$1.00	S
SudAmericana de Vapores, Sailing Cruise Ship, S.S. "Laja"	$10.00	$7.50	$5.00	S
Suncoast, Casino	$2.00	$1.50	$1.00	S
Sunoco, Gas Logo	$8.00	$6.00	$4.00	S
Sunset Station, Casino	$2.00	$1.50	$1.00	S
Superman, Red "S" in Shield	$12.00	$9.00	$6.00	S
Survival, Different Techniques Each Card	$5.00	$4.00	$2.50	S
Swedish American Line, Cruise Lines, Lettering Only	$4.00	$3.00	$2.00	S
Sweetnotes Heart-Shaped Valentines, Two's Company	$8.00	$6.00	$4.00	U
Synovate Consumer Opinion Panel	$1.00	$0.75	$0.50	S
Tampa Bay Buccaneers	$6.00	$4.50	$3.00	S
Tampa Bay Devil Rays	$6.00	$4.50	$3.00	S
Tampa Bay Lightning	$6.00	$4.50	$3.00	S
Taplow's Scotch Whiskey	$10.00	$7.50	$5.00	S
Target, Red Bull's Eye, Department Store	$10.00	$7.50	$5.00	S
Taurus the Bull, Zodiac Sign, 1960s	$10.00	$7.50	$5.00	S
TCA, Fly TCA, The Maple Leaf Route, Maple Leaf in Circle	$5.00	$4.00	$2.50	S
TDC Brand	$2.00	$1.50	$1.00	S
Teenage Mutant Ninja Turtles, 1980s	$8.00	$6.00	$4.00	S
Tenneco, Lettering Only	$3.00	$2.00	$1.50	S
Tennessee Aquarium, Mini Deck, Plastic Case	$3.00	$2.00	$1.50	M
Tennessee State Outline	$2.00	$1.50	$1.00	S
Tennessee Titans	$6.00	$4.50	$3.00	S
Tennessee Volunteers, University	$5.00	$4.00	$2.50	S
Tennessee Volunteers, University, Double Deck Set	$10.00	$7.50	$5.00	DD
Terra-Cotta Xi'an Quin Chinese Warrior Figures, Hong Kong, 1986	$8.00	$6.00	$4.00	S
Texaco, Gas Logo	$6.00	$4.50	$3.00	S
Texaco, Symbol of Worldwide Progress Through Petroleum	$5.00	$4.00	$2.50	S
Texas A & M University	$5.00	$4.00	$2.50	S
Texas Bluebonnet Flower, Tourist	$4.00	$3.00	$2.00	S
Texas Hold'em Brand, Chinese Import	$2.00	$1.50	$1.00	S
Texas Hold'em, Oversize Deck with 3 Bullet Holes, Leather Holster	$12.00	$9.00	$6.00	U
Texas Longhorn Cattle, Tourist	$4.00	$3.00	$2.00	S
Texas Longhorns, University	$5.00	$4.00	$2.50	S
Texas Pacific Lines, Railroad	$6.00	$4.50	$3.00	S
Texas Rangers	$6.00	$4.50	$3.00	S
Texas Station, Casino	$2.00	$1.50	$1.00	S
Thomas Kincade, 2-Deck Set in Cardboard Decorated Art Box	$12.00	$9.00	$6.00	DD
Three Little Pigs, Disney Cartoon, 1950s	$12.00	$9.00	$6.00	S
3M Company, Building	$4.00	$3.00	$2.00	S
3M Company, Large Lettering	$4.00	$3.00	$2.00	S
3M Company, Plaid Background	$4.00	$3.00	$2.00	S
The Three Stooges, Larry, Mo, & Curly	$10.00	$7.50	$5.00	S

The Three Stooges, Double Deck Golf Set in Tin	$12.00	$9.00	$6.00	DD
Thunderbird Hotel & Casino	$2.00	$1.50	$1.00	S
TIA (Trans International Airways)	$8.00	$6.00	$4.00	S
Tia Maria, The Jamaican Liqueur	$10.00	$7.50	$5.00	S
Tiffany, Fancy 2-Deck Set in Blue Box	$30.00	$22.50	$15.00	DD
Tiger Beer	$6.00	$4.50	$3.00	S
Tim Allen, Celebrity Mug Shot	$4.00	$3.00	$2.00	S
Time Magazine, 1962	$40.00	$30.00	$20.00	S
Tiny Decks, Various Floral, Christmas or Geometric Designs	$2.00	$1.50	$1.00	S
Tommy Hilfiger, Designer Clothing	$12.00	$9.00	$6.00	S
Tootsie Roll Shaped Deck, Tootsie Roll Jokers	$8.00	$6.00	$4.00	U
Toronto Blue Jays	$6.00	$4.50	$3.00	S
Toronto Maple Leafs	$6.00	$4.50	$3.00	S
Toronto Raptors	$6.00	$4.50	$3.00	S
Torpedo Brand, Red Cross WWII Issue, 48-Card Pinochle Deck	$12.00	$9.00	$6.00	P
Toulouse Latreo, Piatnik, Double Deck Set	$12.00	$9.00	$6.00	DD
Townsend Thoresen, Cruise Ship	$8.00	$6.00	$4.00	S
Toy Story Animated Movie, I or II, 1990s	$10.00	$7.50	$5.00	S
Transformation, 19th Century French			$750.00	S
Transformers, Robot Toys	$8.00	$6.00	$4.00	S
Traffic Control Technologies	$1.00	$0.75	$0.50	S
Treasure Island, Casino	$2.00	$1.50	$1.00	S
Trolls, Troll Dolls on Each Card	$10.00	$7.50	$5.00	S
Tropicana, Casino	$2.00	$1.50	$1.00	S
Tropicana, Orange Juice Girl	$10.00	$7.50	$5.00	S
TropWorld, Casino	$2.00	$1.50	$1.00	S
Trump Hotel & Casino	$2.00	$1.50	$1.00	S
Trump Regency, Casino	$2.00	$1.50	$1.00	S
Trumps Long Cut, Pin-Up Girls each Card, Tobacco Insert, 1886			$750.00	S
TT Line Clipper, Cruise Boat	$4.00	$3.00	$2.00	S
Tullamore Dew Finest Old Irish Whiskey	$10.00	$7.50	$5.00	S
Tuxedo, Brand	$2.00	$1.50	$1.00	S
TV Magic Cards by Stancraft, 1970s	$4.00	$3.00	$2.00	S
TWA, Carolans Irish Cream Liqueur	$8.00	$6.00	$4.00	S
TWA, Collector Series, Various Jets, 1950s–1960s	$12.50	$10.00	$7.50	S
TWA, Picture of a Lockheed 749 Jet, USPC, 1970	$10.00	$7.50	$5.00	S
TWA, Red & White Jets	$8.00	$6.00	$4.00	S
TWA, Red & White Lettering Top & Bottom, Jet in Middle	$8.00	$6.00	$4.00	S
TWA, Letters in Strip or Globe	$5.00	$4.00	$2.50	S
Two of a Kind	$1.00	$0.75	$0.50	S
UAW-GM (United Auto Workers—General Motors)	$4.00	$3.00	$2.00	S
UCLA, University of California Los Angeles	$5.00	$4.00	$2.50	S
Uncle Sam Brand by Bicycle, 1940s	$12.00	$9.00	$6.00	S
Union Fait la Force, Hitler being Bombed, WWII			$125.00	S
Union Label	$1.00	$0.75	$0.50	S
Union Oyster House, Boston, Double Deck Set, 1950s	$40.00	$30.00	$20.00	DD
Union Pacific, Railroad	$8.00	$6.00	$4.00	S
Union Pacific Railroad, 1910			$75.00	S
Union Plaza Hotel & Casino	$2.00	$1.50	$1.00	S
Union 76, Gas Logo	$6.00	$4.50	$3.00	S
United Air Lines, Various Designs	$4.00	$3.00	$2.00	S
United Airlines, Fly the Friendly Skies	$5.00	$4.00	$2.50	S
United Airlines, Fly the Friendly Skies, Double Deck Set	$10.00	$7.50	$5.00	DD
United Airlines, 1976 Bicentennial	$5.00	$4.00	$2.50	S
United Founders Life Insurance, Building & Rainbow	$4.00	$3.00	$2.00	S
United International, Show World Air Express	$5.00	$4.00	$2.50	S
United States Air Force	$8.00	$6.00	$4.00	S
United States Army	$8.00	$6.00	$4.00	S
United States Army & Navy, USPC, Gold Edge, 1915			$50.00	S
U.S. Army Special Services	$10.00	$7.50	$5.00	S
United States Coast Guard	$8.00	$6.00	$4.00	S
United States Flag	$5.00	$4.00	$2.50	S
United States Lines, S.S. America Cruise Ship	$6.00	$4.50	$3.00	S
United States Lines, S.S. Leviathan Cruise Ship	$10.00	$7.50	$5.00	S
United States Maps, Different Map Each Card	$5.00	$4.00	$2.50	S
United States Marines	$8.00	$6.00	$4.00	S
United States Navy	$8.00	$6.00	$4.00	S
United States Navy Seals	$8.00	$6.00	$4.00	S
United States Special Forces	$8.00	$6.00	$4.00	S
United States Steel Company, USS, Skyscraper	$6.00	$4.50	$3.00	S
Universal Brand, Taiwan	$2.00	$1.50	$1.00	S
Universal Studios	$4.00	$3.00	$2.00	S
University of California, Various Small Branches	$4.00	$3.00	$2.00	S
UNLV Runnin' Rebels, University of Nevada Las Vegas	$5.00	$4.00	$2.50	S
USC, University of Southern California	$5.00	$4.00	$2.50	S
University of Hawaii	$5.00	$4.00	$2.50	S
University of Michigan Football	$4.00	$3.00	$2.00	S
University of Pittsburgh, 1 Joker, 1905 Souvenir Deck		$75.00	$50.00	S
Upper Michigan Copper Country, Mini Deck, Plastic Case	$3.00	$2.00	$1.50	M
USS Constitution, Sailing Ship, Boston	$8.00	$6.00	$4.00	S
Utah Jazz	$6.00	$4.50	$3.00	S
Vail Ski Resort, Colorado	$4.00	$3.00	$2.00	S
Van Camps, Unusual Ace of Spades, 1 Joker, 1911		$100.00	$75.00	S
Vancouver Canucks	$6.00	$4.50	$3.00	S
Vancouver Grizzlies	$6.00	$4.50	$3.00	S
Vanderbilt University	$5.00	$4.00	$2.50	S
Vantage Cigarettes, Various Pack Designs	$6.00	$4.50	$3.00	S
Vargas Girls, Pin-Ups each Card, Starcraft, 1 Joker, 1953			$150.00	S
VAT 69, Scotch Whiskey	$6.00	$4.50	$3.00	S
Vegas Brand	$2.00	$1.50	$1.00	S
Vegas Nite Roulette	$2.00	$1.50	$1.00	S
The Venetian, Hotel & Casino	$2.00	$1.50	$1.00	S
Vermont, Scenic, Tourist	$4.00	$3.00	$2.00	S
Viceroy Cigarettes	$6.00	$4.50	$3.00	S
Victory, Patriot Face Cards (Uncle Sam, etc.), Arrco, 1945		$100.00	$75.00	S

Vienna Melange, Piatnik, Double Deck Set	$12.00	$9.00	$6.00	DD
Vintage Motor Cars	$5.00	$4.00	$2.50	S
Virginia is for Lovers, Tourist	$4.00	$3.00	$2.00	S
Virginia Slims, Cigarettes, Lettering Only	$6.00	$4.50	$3.00	S
Virginia Slims, Cigarettes, Model on Backs	$12.00	$9.00	$6.00	S
Virginia Truckee, Railroad	$6.00	$4.50	$3.00	S
Virgo the Virgin, Zodiac Sign, 1960s	$10.00	$7.50	$5.00	S
Wabash, Follow the Flag, Railroad	$6.00	$4.50	$3.00	S
Waddington, English National Emblems, Unicorn Kings	$15.00	$10.00	$7.50	S
Wall Street Journal	$6.00	$4.50	$3.00	S
Walt Disney World, Various Tourist Designs	$4.00	$3.00	$2.00	S
Walt Disney World, Cinderella Castle	$4.00	$3.00	$2.00	S
Walter Bledsoe Coal Company	$4.00	$3.00	$2.00	S
Washington & Pacific Northwest Railroad, 1900			$125.00	S
Washington Bullets	$6.00	$4.50	$3.00	S
Washington Capitals	$6.00	$4.50	$3.00	S
Washington, D.C., Tourist Deck, 1910			$75.00	S
Washington Monument, Washington, D.C.	$4.00	$3.00	$2.00	S
Washington Redskins	$6.00	$4.50	$3.00	S
Washington Wizards	$6.00	$4.50	$3.00	S
Wasp Brand Playing Cards, 2 Deck Set in Decorated Wood Box	$20.00	$15.00	$10.00	DD
Waterman Line, Cruise Ship	$6.00	$4.50	$3.00	S
Wayne Newton Theater, Branson, Missouri	$4.00	$3.00	$2.00	S
Welch's Grape Juice 2 Deck Set, Niagara & Concord	$10.00	$7.50	$5.00	DD
Werewolf, Creepy Classics Oval Deck	$5.00	$4.00	$2.50	U
West Virginia, Tourist, Take Me Home West Virginia	$4.00	$3.00	$2.00	S
Western, Bird on Plane, The Only Way to Fly	$5.00	$4.00	$2.50	S
Western Airlines, "W" in Square Each End	$5.00	$4.00	$2.50	S
Western Knives	$6.00	$4.50	$3.00	S
Western Maryland, Fast Freight Line, Railroad	$6.00	$4.50	$3.00	S
Western Pacific, Railroad	$6.00	$4.50	$3.00	S
Western Village, Casino	$2.00	$1.50	$1.00	S
Westinghouse, Washer & Dryer	$6.00	$4.50	$3.00	S
Westward Ho, Casino	$2.00	$1.50	$1.00	S
Wheat Chex Cereal	$10.00	$7.50	$5.00	S
Wheels, Brand, Piatnik of Austria	$3.00	$2.00	$1.50	S
Whirlpool Appliances	$4.00	$3.00	$2.00	S
Whist 53 European Style Deck	$4.00	$3.00	$2.00	S
White Horse Scotch Whiskey	$6.00	$4.50	$3.00	S
The White House, Washington, D.C.	$4.00	$3.00	$2.00	S
Wickes Lumber Double Deck Set	$2.00	$1.50	$1.00	DD
Wickuler Beer, 1975	$10.00	$7.50	$5.00	S
Wienermobile, Henry Ford Museum	$4.00	$3.00	$2.00	S
Wild Animal Park, San Diego, California	$4.00	$3.00	$2.00	S
Wild Turkey Bourbon	$8.00	$6.00	$4.00	S
Wild Wild West, Casino	$2.00	$1.50	$1.00	S
Wildfire, Casino	$2.00	$1.50	$1.00	S
Win Lose or Draw Vintage Pinups	$75.00	$50.00	$35.00	S
Winchester Mystery House, San Jose, California	$3.00	$2.00	$1.50	S
Winchester, Rifle, 1929			$350.00	S
Winchester, Super X Ammunition	$15.00	$11.00	$7.50	S
Winchester Western, Mallard Duck in Flight	$8.00	$6.00	$4.00	S
Wings, Cigarettes, 1940s			$50.00	S
Winnie the Pooh, Disney	$8.00	$6.00	$4.00	S
Winnipeg Jets	$6.00	$4.50	$3.00	S
Winston Cigarettes, Various Pack Designs	$6.00	$4.50	$3.00	S
Winston Cigarettes. Double Deck Set	$12.00	$9.00	$6.00	DD
Winston Lights Cigarettes	$6.00	$4.50	$3.00	S
Wisconsin Dells, Rock Formations	$4.00	$3.00	$2.00	S
Wisconsin, 4th House on the Rock	$4.00	$3.00	$2.00	S
The Wisconsin Life Insurance Company	$3.00	$2.00	$1.50	S
Wisconsin, The Dairy State, Cows, Tourist	$4.00	$3.00	$2.00	S
Wizard of Oz, Single Deck In Tin, Two Styles, 1990s Issue	$6.00	$4.50	$3.00	S
Wofford College	$4.00	$3.00	$2.00	S
Wonder Works	$1.00	$0.75	$0.50	S
World Airways, Golden Globe	$6.00	$4.50	$3.00	S
World Poker Tour Brand	$2.00	$1.50	$1.00	S
World Series Poker Tour, Double Deck Set in Tin	$10.00	$7.50	$5.00	DD
World Trade Center, Twin Towers, New York	$12.00	$9.00	$6.00	S
World War II, Anti-Hitler Cartoon Caricatures	$12.00	$9.00	$6.00	S
World War II Aircraft Spotter, Axis & Allies, USPC, 1940s			$250.00	S
Xavier University	$5.00	$4.00	$2.50	S
X-Men, Comics	$8.00	$6.00	$4.00	S
Yellow Freight	$1.00	$0.75	$0.50	S
Yellow Pages	$4.00	$3.00	$2.00	S
Yellowstone National Park	$4.00	$3.00	$2.00	S
Yellowstone Park, Photos of the Park, 1 Joker, 1925		$50.00	$35.00	S
Yu-Gi-Oh Anime	$8.00	$6.00	$4.00	S
Yukon Jack, Liquor	$8.00	$6.00	$4.00	S
Zenith	$6.00	$4.50	$3.00	S
Zesta Saltine Crackers, Keebler, Box Design	$10.00	$7.50	$5.00	S
Zima, Clear Malt Beverage	$6.00	$4.50	$3.00	S
Zodiac Deck by Piatnik	$6.00	$4.50	$3.00	S